Inside Psychotherapy

Inside Psychotherapy

Nine Clinicians Tell How They Work and
What They Are Trying to Accomplish

Edited by
Adelaide Bry

Basic Books, Inc. • Publishers
New York • London

Library of Congress Catalog Number: 74—174808
SBN: 465–03314–8

Manufactured in the United States of America

To Barbara and Douglas

who
I hope
will enjoy living
with all its perils
rise from defeat
and treasure the inexplicable beauties

⊂⊇ *Preface*

THIS book offers the reader a unique opportunity—to meet a variety of leaders in the world of psychotherapy and to hear them tell, in their own words, their theory of human behavior and the technique of psychotherapy that they have evolved from that theory.

The form is unusual in that it is a dialogue; the reader shares with the interviewer the feeling that he is *there.* Many of these men have written in theoretical terms about their philosophies, either in works of their own or as part of other works in this field; few have succinctly directed their beliefs to a concrete examination of how that therapy works in practice.

My goal was to let each psychotherapist talk freely, openly, easily about his own method; many of the therapists told me spontaneously after the interview that they hadn't expected to enjoy it so much! All agreed that a new dimension had been added—the chance to express in concrete terms certain ideas about therapy they might never have said in precisely this way.

Most of the interviews took place in the office of the therapist, where they were recorded directly on tape; it was an environment in which each person was relaxed, and that, too, is an important part of each dialogue. The interviews were edited only for short repetitions, the kind one would find in any easy conversation, and for space, but otherwise each interview is the mark of the man.

The dialogues reveal, too, not only an individual way of thinking about theory and therapy, but also the individual, unmistakable stamp of personality. The reader has the freedom to interpret as he wishes, to feel more sympathetic toward one person or one type of therapy than another, not on the basis of any scientific rationale, but simply on the basis of feeling.

It becomes evident from meeting these therapists at work that regardless of the particular theory, therapy itself is still an art form rather than a science. That conclusion was reinforced as I traveled from one to another. The voyage of self-discovery is a personal search; it is not the same for each therapist, nor for each patient, above and beyond the skill involved and the technique used. Despite tremendous advances in understanding the human psyche, there is, as yet, no *one way*. Psychotherapy offers unlimited possibilities for growth and, at the same time, has realistic limitations.

There are nine types of psychotherapy included in this volume, but there is no slight intended for the types not selected. While there is a wide range here—from classical psychoanalysis to marathon encounter—it is a selective judgment. Other types could well have been included in the rapidly shifting, growing field of psychotherapy.

For me, the interviewing was a fascinating and gratifying experience. I started out initially because of my own curiosity about the varieties of psychotherapy being practiced; I had tried three myself. I was unable to find any book which told me what I wanted to know—what goes on behind the closed door.

I extend my personal thanks to the psychotherapists who opened their doors for these dialogues.

Adelaide Bry

1972

Introduction

Lewis R. Wolberg, M.D.

AN impartial observer of the contemporary psychotherapeutic scene would be forced to admit that present-day theories about how people become emotionally ill are exceeded in number only by the available remedies for making them well again. The individual seeking help for an emotional problem, the student in quest of training in psychotherapy, the investigator searching for answers to the puzzling problems of process and outcome research—all are confronted with an imponderable dilemma of choice. Which psychodynamic systems most reasonably solve the riddle of etiology? And which methods are most effective in bringing the ravages of psychological illness to a halt? Complicating the problem of choice is the fact that many present-day practitioners identified with specific ideologies in psychology have radically altered the original theories to which they are still verbally dedicated. More practically, a good number have wandered far afield from the pristine methods advocated by the founders of their elected school.

The virtue of this present volume is that it provides us with a window into the private treatment chambers of a number of psychotherapists practicing diverse forms of therapy, from classical psychoanalysis to nude marathons. This gives us an opportunity to assess points of similarity and difference in what practitioners say is happening to their patients during therapy and the kinds of interventions they institute.

Reader responses to the different orientations will understandably vary. Certain approaches will make more sense than others. To different readers some techniques will sound productive and potent, some implausible or recondite. A number will have an emotional appeal. The illustrative accounts will be interpreted variously as dramatic, boring, reasonable, ludicrous, enlightening, confusing, educational, puzzling, amusing, shocking, even revolting. While the nonprofessional reader may not have the background to evaluate the validity of the claims for their chosen therapies made by the more enthusiastic contributors, the interviews will provide him with glimpses of the theories and technical processes employed by practitioners of a number of representative schools of psychiatry and psychology. In "off-the-cuff" interviewing, therapeutic operations are perhaps more lucidly and vividly described than they would be in a carefully written exegesis.

Obviously one cannot take all of the statements made at their face value. Conservative opinions about their results are rarely voiced by therapists who have originated special treatment approaches, or who have closely identified themselves with particular schools. And perhaps this is how it should be, since a good deal of the impact of psychotherapy is dependent on the enthusiastic conviction the therapist displays in executing his technical operations. Such fervor will in turn inspire faith, hope, and trust in the patient, helping to restore his sense of mastery. Pragmatic as this may prove to be, from a scientific research point of view it is a liability. So many things happen in psychotherapy, that it is difficult to differentiate how much of the patient's improvement is due to the specific tactics of a designated therapeutic system, and how much to nonspecific intercurrent, auxiliary agencies that have little to do with the theoretical and methodological premises of the system. If we make allowances for the zeal of the contributors, and for the global overstatements of some of them, we may nevertheless mine from this volume some precious ore that can enrich our understanding of contemporary trends in the psychotherapeutic field.

A question that confounds us at the start in evaluating the effectiveness of the different psychotherapies is why all of the existing procedures seem to work, not only from the statements of the respective therapists but also the verdicts of their patients, the latters' relatives and friends, and even impartial observers. Surely there must be common healing factors that come into play in the course of a helping process that prosecute change, and that are not explicitly described in the theories of the systems.

All therapists make theoretical assumptions about how and why their strategies work, which may or may not coordinate with the existing facts. An outstanding example of this is the commentary in the chapter on nude marathon therapy of its goal. The object in this therapy, we are told, is regression to the womb, and the techniques employed—immersion in a warm pool, rocking, silence—are presumed to reproduce this condition. Yet in the eloquent description of the management of a phobia, one may recognize a host of healing agencies that suggest over-simplification of the regressive explanation. By the same token some of the chapters on the more conventional systems provide interpretations that sound equally remote. Multiple vectors that enter into therapy seem to be neglected in favor of a unitary and limited hypothesis. The great variety of theories available today might lead us to the conclusion that at least one of them must be right. The question is: "Which one?" The resolution of this moot point is difficult because practically no practitioner affiliated with a distinctive school of psychology will admit openly that there is even a chance that he is wrong.

Yet experienced therapists, in reporting certain facts about what they do and what is going on in their patients, are not entirely blind. Their sight may be blurred by their theories, and their focus limited. This may convince them of the fact that while they are reporting accurately a mere particle of a complex mosaic, the total therapeutic gestalt is more or less obscured.

A principal and universally accepted assumption in the gestalt of psychotherapy is that the presenting problems or symptoms are in a significant way related either to past learning or developmental defects, or to present-day environmental difficulties that tax beyond tolerance the existing coping resources. Another assumption is that we may, through propitious learning experiences, within the matrix of certain techniques, influence the individual toward a better life adaptation. A minimum goal in such efforts is cessation of the current stress situation and alleviation of symptoms. A maximal objective is the reconstruction of the personality structure itself so that it may endure greater hardships and promote a more creative life style.

Toward these ends a luxuriant group of methodologies present themselves, each with an elaborate theoretical structure around which special techniques are organized. Accordingly, various schools of psychotherapy have been organized, usually by charismatic leaders who attract a large body of followers. If the leader is tolerant and flexible, he will tend, as he tests his assumptions, to alter his theories and techniques; he may even tolerate deviations among his group. If he is rigid and conceives of his offerings as transcendental, he will repudiate any change and banish deviants from his established system. Since research stems from dissatisfaction with existing paradigms, a scientific inquiry into a sacrosanct system may be discouraged, or only those findings from incidental research accepted which support the doctrine of the system.

For many years psychotherapy has aimlessly strayed, in the opinion of empirically-minded observers, into becoming an unhealthy collage of murky concepts. Such sceptics have insisted that only through painstaking research can it be brought from its isolated drift into the family of sciences. This happy objective would necessitate applying to psychotherapy the methods of science in order to break it up into lawful sequences. Involved in scientific method are a number of basic operations. We, first, pose a question. Second, we gather data. Third, we make observations about this data from which we elaborate inferences or generalizations. Fourth, we contrive predictions. Fifth, we compile new observations which either support or repudiate our predictions. One frequently used means of approach is molar or holistic; here we decide not to tamper with the phenomena under study, but rather to mull over it in its existing state. This is the "field of observation method." The second, commonly employed kind of approach is to select a small group of variables, keeping the others as constant as possible, and then set up experiments to confirm or negate our predictions. This is generally known as the "experimental or molecular method." In order to help us pinpoint significant factors, we employ "controls," hoping by this means to reduce error. The reliability of assessments is enhanced by utilizing the judgments of a group of experienced and specialized observers ("judges") who independently view the data. We furthermore attempt to reduce error by compiling as many observations as possible and by the use of proper statistical procedures.

Since psychotherapy involves a bewildering number of variables which are difficult to control, and since many of these variables change through time, the results of current research has been anything but spectacular. Studies of the content of sessions, personality characteristics of patients who respond best to set techniques, personality features of therapists who appear to get the best and poorest results in therapy, the effect of drugs on interview content, and the prediction of outcome in therapy have yielded a number of interesting hypotheses that still await proper retesting. The indications are that ultimately we shall be able more precisely to apply to the data of psychotherapy, the methods of empirical research. In the meantime we may have no alternative other than to listen to the accounts of participant observers, such as in the interviews recorded in this volume.

The question that will naturally occur is whether a clinician can view his own data impartially as a scientist. When we consider the complexities of practice in psychotherapy, not the least of which are its economics and the status competition of professionals, we may not give greatest credence to all of the pronouncements of its enthusiastic practitioners. It would be obviously unfair to expect any professional to be completely objective about what he is doing when enthusiasm about his method is an ingredient in influencing his patient toward cure. This does not mean that we must accept without challenge what he has to say.

Examining critically the content of the interviews in this book, they appear on the surface to be worlds apart in theory and method. On closer investigation we observe many similarities. We may take as an analogy a group of people coming from different countries, each of whom speaks a different language. Their observations of a specific happening to which they have all been simultaneously exposed will be comprehensible in spoken or written form only to persons who understand the corresponding dialect. Yet they will essentially be saying much of the same thing in what will seem like a babel of tongues. There will also be novel judgments, conclusions, and solutions offered, depending on each observer's unique education, experience, and value system. But even here we may discern some common similarities.

This analogy is not too remote if we consider that all psychotherapeutic techniques are forms of communication through which important influencing processes operate. For the techniques to be effective the patient and therapist must understand each other's language. Coordinately, it is vital that the patient feel an affinity for the theories and methods around which the therapist is organizing his treatment. He will then figuratively be on the same wave length as his therapist. It is important also that the therapist be firmly dedicated to his approach so that confidence in what he is doing comes through to his patient and keeps alive the latter's faith.

In all therapies, once communication is established, a number of nonspecific helping factors precipitate out. The patient, distraught by his symptoms or dissatisfied with his adjustment, comes to an expert authority who, he hopes, will lead him to a better existence. Temporarily dependent on this figure in his plea for help, he is bound to project onto him idealized protective and benevolent qualities. The fact that he has dependently put his trust and fate into the hands of a knowledgeable person will make him somewhat more suggestibly susceptible to the explanations and pronouncements of this person. If the therapist's viewpoints coordinate with his education and capacities for conceptualization, he will be more or less inclined to endorse a profered theory and its coordinate techniques. If he accepts and trusts the healing authority, the therapeutic process will have begun.

Almost from the start a number of subsidiary forces will come into play. Not the least of these is the placebo factor, the ubiquitous idolatry extended toward the methods of the healer that may have an almost magical influence on symptoms. In both physical and psychological medicine the placebo effect accounts for a good deal of the initial improvement. The powers of the placebo, the reassuring influence of dependency on the idealized and protective authority figure, and the subsidies of suggestion inherent in the dependent relationship are supplemented by the relief the patient experiences in talking openly about his troubles. Emotional catharsis, issuing from verbal exposure of hidden pockets of fear, grief, and shame, momentarily relieves tension. But the fact that the patient is enabled to talk about his fears and frustrations to an authority who does not respond with expected ridicule or retribution enables the patient to develop a less punitive attitude toward his suppressed secrets. As he puts undefined feelings into words, he tends to reconceptualize and to relabel them. He becomes less defensive about his past. The incorporated image of harsh authority softens.

In all forms of therapy there is a tendency to confuse the new authority as vested in the therapist with the old parental authority toward whom ambivalent attitudes exist. Such transference feelings may never be openly expressed, but they may subtly reveal themselves in dreams, nonverbal behavior and acting-out. Therapists who are untrained in or who minimize psychoanalytic formulations may neglect to search for transference phenomena or to attempt to by-pass it. It will nevertheless operate as an important force in all therapies, enhancing some aspects of the therapeutic process and acting as resistance to others. The ability of the patient to recognize how he projects distortions onto the therapist will serve as one of the most important vehicles for intrapsychic change, often resulting in more or less extensive alterations of the superego and ego structures. Such recognition may occur as undercurrent insights that the patient may never, as has been said before, verbalize openly, especially to a therapist who focuses on realistic aspects of the patient's life.

The therapist's capacity to deal with manifestations of transference when they occur, to interpret them to the patient in terms he can understand, or to behave in ways that remove them as resistance may be the most crucial strategems in his therapeutic stance. Even in psychotherapy that deviates from the conventional psychoanalytic model, this may prove to be the most important means of establishing a therapeutic relationship. Dr. Ross Speck, in his chapter on Family Therapy, speaks of the therapist's practiced avoidance of behavior that mirrors the behavior of family authorities. This, says Speck, may bring the patient to a different conceptualization of himself. An illustration is an early interview with a family in which the principal patient was a twenty-eight-year-old schizophrenic girl. Shabbily attired, she sat in a corner and raised her dress over her head. A family member commented: "Well, Doc, look at her, she's *crazy*." Dr. Speck replied: "I don't know that she's crazy; she looks like an all-American girl to me." He comments then: "With that, a moment later, I saw the edge of the dress come creeping down; an eye appeared, and I even saw a grin on her face. . . . her thoughts, no matter how fragmented, were already turning in the direction of 'Hey, what's going on here? Here's somebody who thinks maybe somebody in the family is nuts *besides* me,' and there's the beginning of a relationship."

In all forms of therapy resistance will appear in stark or disguised forms and may block or destroy therapeutic progress. Despite the fact that his suffering is intense and his symptoms disabling, the patient may resist changing his way of life. Toward this end he may block the efforts of even an experienced therapist. The bounties he derives from pursuing a course that must inevitably result in anxiety and turmoil may not be apparent on the surface. He seems frozen into unreasonable bad habits which he refuses to dissolve. And he may credit his failure to the impotence of his therapist and the worthlessness of the latter's methods. Resistance to change can paralyze all forms of therapy and the capacity to recognize the subtleties and to deal with them constructively spell the difference in any psychotherapeutic endeavor between a therapeutic triumph or a debacle.

What we seem to be dealing with in all of our patients is their *readiness for change*, which apparently involves the degree to which they have spontaneously or with professional help resolved their resistance to change. An individual with reasonable readiness to move forward will seem to benefit from almost any situation or tactic that he can use constructively. It will act for him as the last rung in a ladder, enabling him to step onto a platform of health. For years he may have silently been building the lower rungs, either by himself through spontaneous insights and propitiously reinforcing life experiences, or in formal therapy, which he may abandon before his ladder has been completed, with few apparent signs of improvement. He may then unjustifiably credit his cure entirely to a later therapeutic experience, however brief or coincidental it may be, or to some dramatic event in his life that actually has served as a convenience that he has resourcefully manipulated. As Dr. Hart expressed it in his chapter on Jungian therapy: "I've had people come only three or four times and a whole life problem seems to have been resolved just in time because they were ripe for bringing it out. . . . or I work with people for years perhaps, and then it begins to happen more slowly." Speaking of alcoholics Dr. Hart continues: "I have found real success where the person himself was at a point where he was ready to make a real change and not so much success at another point."

It will be apparent in reading the book that beyond the confines of the prescribed methods of an adopted therapeutic system, the overt maneuvers and strategies of the different therapists will vary greatly, involving such dimensions as (1) the *activity* of the therapist (ranging from greater activity than that shown by the patient, even of dominance, to relative detachment and interpersonal remoteness); (2) the *gratification of demands and impulses* (from intimate involvement, like touching, to outright frustration and denial of the simplest stipulations); (3) the degree of *support and advice* (from outright taking over of all or most decisions, to refusal to offer even indirect suggestions as to alternative courses of action); (4) the extent of *interpretations* (from depth revelations of unconscious processes for which evidence may or may not exist, to refusal to make any interpretations, leaving these to the patient's discretion); (5) the *quality of communications* (free associations; encouragement of fantasy and dream revelations; focusing on specific areas such as early recollections, significant remembered experiences, and present-day activities and preoccupations); and thoughts and feelings about the therapist rooted in real or transferential illusions. The therapist's activities will obviously influence the direction or course of therapy irrespective of the theoretical premises by which the therapist professes to abide.

This is not to deprecate the virtues of good theory. There is much that we have learned about human behavior, and pioneer thinkers, whose points of view are represented in this book, have contributed much toward a more scientific understanding of personality in operation. It has already been pointed out that each school of psychology is probably dealing with a more or less limited aspect of the grand tableau that constitutes psychological man. Theoretical systems center on special zones of interest to the exclusion of other important aspects, and in certain cases with denial that other aspects even exist. The enthusiasm with which the therapist presents his theories will rub off on the patient, helping to bolster the placebo effect. Without a mutuality of conviction treatment will proceed under a handicap. Under the circumstances one may wonder whether a faulty theory firmly believed by therapist and patient may not serve as well as one grounded in some empirical evidence. There is much documentation to support the fact that if both therapist and patient accept a theory as factual, and then proceed to find proof to substantiate it in the life history and present behavior of the patient, the latter may lose his tensions and restore his psychological balances even though later, after he is functioning well, the theory may impress him as remote. For the time being, when he needed it, the theory served its purpose.

It is not irrelevant to these points to indicate that essential similarities in theory among the varying systems are often masked by differences in emphasis. For example, the principle of making the unconscious conscious by lifting repressions is the aim of all of the psychoanalytic therapies described in this book. Dr. Hammet delineates the Freudian position this way: "The ingredients of psychic illness operate largely in the *unconscious*. It's only by virtue of their *being* unconscious that they can cause illness. We believe that if they are conscious they lose their pathogenic properties." Dr. Hart confirms the fact that in the Jungian approach the unconscious is also held to be responsible for psychic illness; however what is repressed are not pathological conflicts, but healthy *unconscious* energies which are always striving for realization. Dr. Singer, explaining Eric Fromm's approach, states that what is essential is an exposure of more or less *unconscious* "basic realistic tendencies." Dr. Perls in his gestalt therapy exposes the *unconscious* repudiated parts of the self to confront the person with his façades and defenses. In all of the approaches the aim is to make the unconscious conscious, through verbalizations, role playing, dreams and other symbolic types of expression.

While a radically different tactic is described by Wolpe under Behavior Therapy, one would suspect that many of the same healing processes go on in the conditioning approaches as in other approaches. The focus is on discovering and removing, by behavioral techniques, the foci of anxiety. There is a probing, says Wolpe, among other things, of the "early home life, relationships with parents. . . . We also give the patient certain questionnaires which reveal areas of disturbance that he may not even have mentioned. . . ." Are they not mentioned because the patient has rejected, suppressed, or forgotten them? We might suspect that they have been relegated to areas of the psyche of which the individual is purposefully, for the moment, unaware. Some observers would conceive of this as operations of various levels of the vast brain-storage system, which includes the unconscious. As far as the encounter therapies are concerned, exposure of unconscious conflicts and feelings comes about constantly as a result of a frontal attack on resistances.

When we cut through the semantics we may all be talking about the same phenomena but stressing different aspects of it. This is brought out in a question about the essence of psychotherapy. Dr. Hammet replies: It is "more than anything else, a way to find out about yourself." Dr. Hart insists: "I guess it's respect for the whole person or for the psyche, and the wholeness which is striving to be realized." Dr. Singer's statement explicating the Frommian neo-Freudian slant is not incompatible with these viewpoints. The therapeutic process, he states, is "progressively expanding personal self-knowledge." Dr. Perls defines what happens as exposing and then reassimilating the repudiated aspects of self: "The core of therapy is learning to confront your opposites." Dr. Stoller implies that the objective of encounter groups is the expansion of self-awareness.

When we come to the actual technical operations of assorted therapists we find that there are even more similarities. Thus, despite wide theoretical differences in psychoanalytic theories, the practice of psychoanalysis is relatively unified. Indeed differences here are often indistinguishable. This is clearly brought out in Dr. Singer's chapter, describing Eric Fromm's position. Freud is criticized for his continuous insistence upon man in constant search of stimulus-avoidance, always eager to find a homeostatic state, and his viewing his achievements—limited and dangerous as some may be—as remarkable sublimations of essentially regressive striving." Singer continues with his ideas: "Man's reason makes him capable of painfully anticipating the end of his reason, his own death. Furthermore the inherent problem is man's ability to recognize his relative insignificance . . . his essential aloneness." One will see in this thought a definite bent toward an existential philosophy. Yet when asked how this applies to the way psychoanalytic interventions are implemented, Singer says that when he does therapy "I become a Freudian." Among the more active behavioral and encounter therapies, many modes of functioning are also remarkably unified.

How the patient responds to our therapeutic tactics is intrinsically bracketed to the type of individual with whom we are dealing. There are an endless number of patient variables which will augment or negate specific technical operations. Space allows mention of only a few. For instance, the degree of existing personality dependence of the patient is an important factor in his potential response. Dependency may either be a product of the current collapse of defenses with emergence of childish helplessness, or reveal itself as an aspect of the prevailing character structure. In the former case we may expect a rapid return to a more mature autonomous functioning once stress is alleviated. In the latter instance we may have to point our efforts toward personality reconstruction before significant progress can be made. The degree of his trustingness is related to other existing personality factors, such as detachment, hostility and dependence. The inability to develop trust in the relationship may interfere with the emergence of the proper therapeutic climate. Less apparent is the severity of damaging unconscious conflicts, for example, between impulses and one's conscience, that have been repressed and repudiated, and the persistence of repertoires of past behaviors and expressions of childish needs. The degree of anxiety investing such conflicts and behaviors, and the intensity of repression that dissociates the conflicts from awareness, will often determine the destiny of the therapeutic effort. An understanding by the therapist of the significance of the unconscious, and skill in making available to the patient symbolic tokens that he can tolerate, will help expedite the proper focusing of therapy.

A factor that may determine the effectiveness of a special technique is the particular kind of problem or situation for which help is being sought. Obviously, if a person who has habitually made a good adjustment encounters a situational crisis with which he is unable to cope, he will do better with an active short-term approach, geared to the immediate resolution of his environmental difficulty and his symptoms, than he will with a long-term depth-oriented approach, focused on his intrapsychic processes. Conversely, an individual with persistent, urgent, compulsive and repetitive drives, issuing from unresolved childish needs, who is constantly immersed in a sea of troubles, and applies for help because he feels himself drowning, will probably benefit much more from long-term reconstructive insight-oriented management, than from the more dramatic experiential and behavioral therapies. This is not to say that he might not rapidly benefit from the latter. However, the chances are that his healthy accruals will rapidly be deluged by the neurotic demands of his inner conflicts which will over and over again plunge him into misery.

Certain techniques seem to be tailor-made for designated problems and situations. Phobic disorders, for example, have yielded more rapidly to behavior therapy, executed by an experienced therapist, than to any other form of treatment. The addictions (drug, alcohol, food) are peculiarly resistive to formal individual psychotherapy, but do respond better to group approaches (Synanon, Alcoholics Anonymous, Weight Watchers). Tension states are often quickly brought to a halt with hypnosis. Encounter groups seem designed for the person who is isolated and detached, for one who has been described as "the person who has trouble reaching out to people and allowing himself to be touched by people."

What we are concerned with essentially are the goals toward which our treatment effort is being directed. Symptom relief? Situational alterations? Character changes? Some of the approaches are better suited for certain objectives than for others. Dr. Stoller, in his chapter on "Encounter Groups" explicitly refers to this fact when he defines the difference between a therapeutic and an encounter group. The former is geared toward exploring symptoms and problems, discovering the "why" of one's troubles. The latter is oriented around providing for the person a living experience: "getting in touch with yourself at a much richer level than you might have otherwise."

A legitimate concern is whether the professed goals of a therapeutic system are actually realized in practice. Do reconstructive therapies, like psychoanalysis, truly bring about extensive alterations of the personality; and do the symptom-oriented therapies uniformly relieve symptoms? There has been no scientific validation of these facts even though the hunch is that they are substantially correct. The *potentials* for personality growth are present in reconstructive therapy, properly conducted by an experienced therapist who applies it to a receptive patient under circumstances that are propitious for growth. And symptom-oriented therapies do help relieve emotional problems, often quite dramatically. But there are important exceptions. Sometimes, even under the guidance of skillful analysts who have been properly trained, some patients, after having been in therapy for years, achieve mere symptom relief and never proceed on to enjoy the fruits of a reconstructive harvest. Other patients, briefly seen by behavior therapists will show, in addition to relief of symptoms, a surprising growth in personality maturation. A readiness for change is obviously there. And some individuals acquire a readiness for change without the intervention of any formal therapy, and, in a suitable environment, may reverse patterns acquired through unfortunate conditionings as far back as early childhood. This development is a product of constructive relearning, which is, after all, what psychotherapy is all about.

The reader may get the impression that with all of the variables that are operative in therapy, the actual techniques to which patients are exposed are of relatively little importance. This is not true. The techniques are *the communicative means* through which healing forces are set into operation. They provide a basis for constructive relearning. People learn best through selective channels. Some will learn advantageously by free association; some by examining dreams; some within an insight group made up of strangers; some by interactions with family members in family therapy; some by the more active behavioral, psychodramatic and encounter techniques. This would seem to make it vital for the therapist to fashion his approach to fit the needs and learning propensities of his patients, rather than to attempt to wedge all of his patients into a circumscribed approach. Because learning patterns are so unique and methods of learning so varied, a good teacher must have at his disposal a good variety of teaching materials.

Here we must deal with the personality of the therapist as a teacher. His sensitivity, perceptiveness and intelligence are, of course, important, but what is equally important, and too often overlooked, is his flexibility—his willingness to challenge the credenda of his accepted system. It is my conviction that this failing accounts for a good number of failures in psychotherapy, failures generally credited to the obstinacy, lack of motivation, and ego weakness of the patient. Flexibility does not mean an undisciplined casting to the winds of structure in psychotherapy, or acting out with the patient in response to his provocations. It does imply an ability to adapt to the patient's immediate emotional needs and to design an approach in accordance with the patient's abilities to learn.

Flexibility of approach implies acceptance of the principle of eclecticism of method. Too often eclecticism is regarded as a heretical compromise, a monstrosity born of the wedlock of expediency and opportunism. Self-appointed bearers of the scientific torch are whipped into a fury at the very sound of the word. Readers of this volume dedicated to precepts of technological purity will, undoubtedly, regard with disdain activities during the treatment hour such as are described by Ross Speck who in Family Therapy does not hesitate to employ role-playing, psychodrama, and various forms of nonverbal communication: "You ask the family members to touch each other, change seats, move around the office, sit on the floor." Speck even makes home visits. Employing different kinds of chairs, he says, "I use these chairs and play detective."

Dr. Speck explains why he avoids a psychoanalytic approach. "The basic job is to loosen up the old structure.... I worked on resistances, defenses, and transference with each member of the family. It was too long, too slow. It may be necessary in certain obsessional types of schizophrenic persons, or serious character disorders or deep neuroses. In the vast majority of families, a direct approach like we've been talking about brings about some change in the first ten sessions. . . . You're not going for *insight*. You're not going for understanding the structural aspects of the mental apparatus or how the defenses operate. You're trying to get change going in *one* family member. Once you do, the theory, like the domino theory, is when the change starts, the others must change. . . . I'll make concrete suggestions about jobs, about moving out of the home, about . . . almost anything. . . . Sometimes when I see a stiff and rigid family after they've seated themselves, I just lie down on the floor and look up at the ceiling."

I personally admire Dr. Speck's originality and his refreshing thrusts toward activity, but I would caution about generalizing that active methods are applicable to the operations of all therapists. There are psychotherapists who are characterologically passive, for whom such techniques would be highly artificial. And their patients would feel the lack of genuineness and fail to respond. For such therapists traditional passive methods will work best because they can be sincerely applied as part of the therapist's true personality in operation.

Not all methods make sense to nor will work for all therapists. A highly discriminating process generally takes place as therapists gain experience and find that certain theories and special techniques seem effective in their hands. A problem that plagues our field, of course, is the tendency to apply one's personal experience to the world at large. The fact that a therapist finds an insight approach of little value for him does not mean that other therapists will do likewise.

In my years of experience as Director of the Postgraduate Center for Mental Health, I have seen many therapists who get extraordinary results with a psychoanalytically oriented approach. The same therapists get nowhere attempting to utilize behavioral or hypnotic techniques. On the other hand we have some Fellows who have gone through a thorough psychoanalytic training course whose results with patients leave much to be desired. Some of these professionals have experimented with encounter, behavioral, or philosophic approaches and have done remarkably well. Their psychoanalytic training was of service only as a way of understanding better how the patient was relating to them and their tactics, as well as enabling them to deal better with their own countertransference. But the methods they found valuable to their particular style of functioning deviated drastically from the psychoanalytic model. This does not mean that what they were doing was iconoclastic. It means that they were better able to relate themselves to their patients through the medium of tactical operations that coordinated with their special personality needs.

In summary, the multiple problems of psychotherapy will never be resolved until we can institute a free interchange of ideas with colleagues from all of the behavioral sciences. Empirical studies are kept alive by infusions of new and original ideas. They are enriched by contributions of those who are willing to experiment with formulations and tactics that deviate from traditional modes, and who are also willing to expose their thoughts and operations for critical review. Unfortunately, in the field of mental health there have been relatively few practitioners with courage enough to put their heads on the chopping block by challenging orthodoxy. Some of these while repeating the catechism of accepted credos for the benefit of their associates, do admit in off-the-record comments a disagreement with original doctrines. But we are confronted too frequently with the frightening spectacle of men so committed to their beliefs that they refuse to relinquish them even when evidence proves that they are wrong.

Dr. Ian Alger, who classifies himself as a psychoanalyst strikes a resonant experimental chord in his chapter when he says: "I've been doing many different things. . . . It's all connected to ways of trying to increase a person's awareness of reality. . . . In this way you create more of an investigative attitude toward yourself and others. This is the atmosphere I create in groups, in therapy and in life, too: a connection with people which says I am interested, I understand and see what is happening." Perhaps this chord will some day evolve melodies that will blend into a symphony of truly effective techniques in psychotherapy.

Contents

Inside Psychotherapy

Van Buren O. Hammett, M.D.

is Chairman of the Department of Psychiatry at Hahnemann Medical College in Philadelphia, a post to which he was appointed in 1958. He is also a member of the consulting staff of the Institute of the Pennsylvania Hospital. He is a member of the American Psychoanalytic Association, and past president of the Philadelphia Psychiatric Society. He is a fellow of the American College of Psychiatrists, the American College of Physicians, and many other societies.

However, Dr. Hammett is not an "ivory tower" psychoanalyst. He is currently concerned with helping to develop psychiatry's role in meeting the need for services related to mental health, and in the training of professionals and paraprofessionals competent to provide these much needed services. As part of this very real involvement, he is a member of the Board of Directors of the Eastern Mental Health Center and of the Central Philadelphia Health Services.

Adelaide Bry ◆ Dr. Hammett, does a psychoanalyst differ from a psychiatrist? These two words often get confused.

Dr. Hammett ◆ Yes, they do. A psychoanalyst ordinarily is a psychiatrist, but he has in addition taken specialized training in psychoanalysis, which is a subspecialty of psychiatry.

A. B. ◆ What does that training consist of?

Dr. Hammett ◆ It's quite comprehensive and extensive. First, like all analysts, I had a personal analysis. One must have a personal analysis which is usually a rather long and searching one. Then there are courses—formally organized lectures and seminars on theory and technique of psychoanalysis. Finally, the trainee must do four cases, patients, whom he analyzes under the supervision of one of his teachers.

A. B. ◆ What is the theory of psychoanalysis?

Dr. Hammett ◆ I can't answer it in a few words. But here are the salient points. Psychoanalysis places great emphasis upon the importance of the unconscious as a factor in mental functioning. That's not unique to psychoanalysis—other schools do too—but psychoanalysis especially emphasizes this.

A. B. ◆ The unconscious—is that the part of your mind that you don't know about?

Dr. Hammett ◆ It's by far and away the largest and most active part of your mind. It's never idle for a moment. You are not aware of it, however. That's why we say unconscious. Unconscious is in contradistinction to conscious, or what we are aware of.

A. B. ◆ You mean that parts of me are going on functioning and making me do certain things that I'm unaware of?

Dr. Hammett ◆ Constantly. To all psychoanalysts this is a fact beyond doubt (and to most psychiatrists). The reason that psychoanalysis emphasizes the unconscious is that according to psychoanalytic theory the ingredients of psychic illness operate largely in the unconscious. It's only by virtue of their *being* unconscious that they can cause illness. We believe that if they are conscious they lose their pathogenic properties, and can no longer make the person ill.

A. B. ♦ No matter how many problems I had, if I were *deeply aware* of my unconscious, then I would not become mentally ill?

Dr. Hammett ♦ Up to that point beyond which even the most competent human being would succumb. There is such a thing as overwhelming stress, but that's a very extraordinary circumstance. It doesn't occur very often in many people's lives. So, the answer to your question is "Yes."

A. B. ♦ I see. That's the theory of psychoanalysis . . .

Dr. Hammett ♦ Well, there is a lot more to it than that. We think that the cause of psychic illness is that there is a disagreement within the person's mind, between certain things. For example, instinctual urges which for one reason or another aren't acceptable to him or to society.

A. B. ♦ Such as . . .

Dr. Hammett ♦ An undeveloped sexual instinct, let's say, such as the urge to look at, or to exhibit oneself, or some of the aggressive impulses. Wanting to hurt or injure someone is an instinctual impulse that is rejected by the individual's conscience, if he has that in his make-up, or if not by his conscience, certainly by society.

A. B. ♦ So he wants to do this thing, but he can't. That puts an extra burden on him.

Dr. Hammett ♦ It creates a conflict for him. He has a war going on within himself between the urge to do it and the fear of doing it, or the disapproval of doing it.

A. B. ♦ And then this war can create anything from what one might call a mild neurosis to actually becoming psychotic.

Dr. Hammett ✦ Yes. All of us, by the way, have some of these repressed, unacceptable, instinctual urges because none of us are completely mature.

A. B. ✦ No, I know I do. I feel some all the time.

Dr. Hammett ✦ We all do. We wouldn't be human if we didn't. But in order to handle these things in ourselves we have what is called in psychoanalytic theory "defense mechanisms." These are ways of functioning mentally which serve the purpose of counteracting or keeping under control undesirable, immature, instinctual impulses.

A. B. ✦ How would that work—if you wanted to hurt somebody?

Dr. Hammett ✦ One common defense mechanism takes the form of developing to a high degree exactly the opposite tendency, so that a person who is chronically filled with rage and has an impulse to go around hitting people would, if he uses this mechanism of defense, develop just the opposite kind of personality. He'd be very courteous, very concerned about other people's well-being, and everyone would say of this person: "My, isn't he thoughtful and gentle."

A. B. ✦ Would it hurt him to behave that way? That sounds just fine.

Dr. Hammett ✦ No. Lots of *good* results come from defense mechanisms unless the quantities of energy that are invoked are excessive. If the defense described has to be built up to the point that it really interferes with the person's effective functioning, he may become too timid because of this, which is a handicap to him.

A. B. ✦ Then at that point he probably should seek professional help . . .

Dr. Hammett ✦ At that point he needs help. This leads directly to the psychoanalytic method of treatment because we have the conflict and the defense that we've been talking about. It is in the mind unconsciously. The individual doesn't know of it and it is producing symptoms in the form of anxiety or any one of many symptoms.

A. B. ✦ What would be some of the other symptoms?

Dr. Hammett ✦ Compulsions or obsessions. For example, the person with chronic rage might develop a compulsion to wash his hands over and over and over again, as a defense against his rage. Recall "Macbeth"; it's trying to wash off the guilt. But, of course, he wouldn't be conscious of his reasons for washing his hands. He would be compelled to wash his hands many times a day, and if he didn't, he would become very uneasy.

A. B. ✦ So this is really the unconscious expressing itself in real life, but you don't know the reason for it.

Dr. Hammett ✦ The symptom does two things. In a disguised way it expresses what is repressed, and it also helps to keep it repressed.

A. B. ✦ But a person could go on washing his hands a lot for the next forty years as long as he was still able to go to business, marry, and have children—lead a life.

Dr. Hammett ✦ That's right.

A. B. ✦ But then there's that other point at which it interferes, and at which the person should have help, and then what happens?

Dr. Hammett ✦ If he goes to a psychoanalyst, the first essential to begin recovery from his illness is that he become aware of what the problem is within his mind. What is repressed in his mind must somehow be brought into consciousness. This is a crucial point in psychoanalytic theory, and it's from this point that the method has developed, because the method of psychoanalytic treatment is built around the idea of helping the patient to *unrepress* and *bring into consciousness* what he needs to know, in order to deal with it in a more sensible and realistic way.

A. B. ✦ What happens if I came to your office for the very first time to consult you as a psychoanalyst? Do I sit down in a chair near your desk? Do I lie on a couch? How do the first few sessions work?

Dr. Hammett ✦ You would sit in a chair and we would talk to one another pretty much the way one does in a social situation. We would just have a conversation about what had brought you to my office, what were your reasons for coming, something of the history of it, when it began, how long you had had it, what things you thought had precipitated it, and perhaps something about your family, your social life, and that sort of thing.

A. B. ✦ How long does that take?

Dr. Hammett ✦ Two, three, four, five hours.

A. B. ✦ And then, after we've gone through this initial stage, how does the treatment start?

Dr. Hammett ✦ If I had by this time decided that you should be treated by psychoanalysis . . .

A. B. ✦ You might decide otherwise?

Dr. Hammett ✦ I might, indeed, decide otherwise. Not all things are best treated by psychoanalysis. I want to emphasize that. Not all kinds of emotional illness are suitable for treatment by analysis. But if I had decided that it would be the best thing for you, I would tell you. I would give you some idea of what this entailed in the way of time and effort on your part, and the expenses.

A. B. ✦ A lot, I guess!

Dr. Hammett ✦ Originally, psychoanalysis meant a daily session, usually for an hour, or as it has come to be in this country, fifty minutes. This is purely a matter of convenience and arranging schedules. There is nothing magical about one hour or fifty minutes. It's just that in order to arrange his schedule in some reasonably, orderly way, a doctor does that. It could be forty minutes. It could be an hour and a half. Usually, it's about an hour.

A. B. ✦ I thought the fifty minute hour was for him to have time in between patients.

Dr. Hammett ✦ He should have a little time in between to catch his breath, perhaps make a few notes and so on. Originally, psychoanalysts saw their patients every day, six days a week in the beginning. After the two-day week-end took hold, it was changed to five days a week. Classical analysts in this country still see the patient five times weekly. Some of us, however, after experience and some experimentation, have reduced this. I will do analysis with three visits a week with the patient; as a matter of fact, I rarely any longer ask a patient to come every day.

A. B. ✦ What was the original reason for the five days a week? Was that what Freud did?

Dr. Hammett ✦ Yes. He experimented at first and tried different things and ways of doing it. It was felt that it was necessary to get a sort of momentum in the work, that it shouldn't be lost once it had been obtained, and that if a patient stayed away for two or three or four days, all of his resistances to self-examination would become reestablished.

A. B. ✦ You feel that with three days a week, one can still work at these resistances?

Dr. Hammett ✦ I'm quite convinced of it.

A. B. ✦ You said that some people aren't suitable for psycho-analysis. What kinds of people?

Dr. Hammett ✦ The persons who still have reasonably intact character, what we call ego function, are good candidates. If the individual has an intact ego with knowledge of reality and the ability to distinguish what is real from what's fantasy, a reasonable amount of intelligence, and a reasonable amount of education . . . You see, the medium of exchange is conversation, talk. It's words. So that a person does have to be reasonably verbal. I'd say that anyone with a couple of years of high school education would qualify in this respect. People who are sicker than this, who have decompensated, whose ego functions are no longer effective, are not suitable for psychoanalysis. These would ordinarily be psychotic individuals.

A. B. ✦ Psychoanalysis seems possible for somebody who is at least walking around and maintaining some kind of life, even though he might not be in such good shape.

Dr. Hammett ◆ That's right, and I'd say that perhaps a majority of persons who are in analysis are continuing their lives more or less successfully; they are not totally disabled.

A. B. ◆ Are there any kinds of cases that are especially good for psychoanalysis? Such as homosexuals, alcoholics, or any other category?

Dr. Hammett ◆ You just happened to mention two that are rather difficult. I would say that alcoholics especially are very difficult to treat in psychoanalysis. Homosexuals, not so very difficult. There are different types of homosexuality. I think we don't want to get into that; it would lead us too far astray. In general, the symptom neuroses—for example, hysteria, phobic conditions, and obsessive-compulsive neurosis—do well with analysis. Also, character disorders indicate analytic treatment.

A. B. ◆ That just means you're all messed up and don't feel good from day to day?

Dr. Hammett ◆ You don't feel good or you don't get along well in your work, you don't progress and succeed, but you don't know why. Or you're not happy at home with your marriage, without gross symptoms.

The next step in treatment is to explain what psycho-analysis is all about. I would say to the patient that the important thing for us to do is to find out what is below the surface of his mind and that various ways of doing this have been tried, such as hypnosis, the so-called truth drugs, and other ways. I believe as an analyst that for the information to be useful for him in his recovery, he needs to be *aware of it as he obtains it.* The only way to do this is for him to just tell me all his thoughts, any and all of them, no matter whether they seem trivial or silly or have no relationship to his complaints and symptoms. When we are having a session, he should say anything of which he becomes aware. *This is the one basic rule.*

A. B. ◆ Nothing else. Does the patient now then lie down on the traditional couch, and do you sit behind him?

Dr. Hammett ◆ Yes—there are advantages to that. One is purely practical: it's a little more comfortable for both the patient and the doctor. You know, unless people are very fond of one another, or unless they're fighting, it's easier not to have to watch one another all the time while talking.

A. B. ◆ I never thought of that before.

Dr. Hammett ◆ It's more relaxed to just talk without watching the other person's face to see how you're being received, and this, incidentally, is the main reason for asking the patient to lie down and not see the doctor: so that he won't watch the doctor's face and change his thoughts according to what he sees or thinks he sees in the way of reaction in the doctor's face. So we try to remove that distraction, and the way we do this is to have the patient lie down, looking at the ceiling.

A. B. ◆ He's doing what Freud called "free association."

Is it possible to express your thoughts as fast as they come? Most of us seem to have an awful lot of thoughts and we only get a few of them out in words.

Dr. Hammett ◆ Yes, it's possible. I think one can express them as fast as they come except occasionally, when they just come rushing. The difficulty that most patients have is not that of expressing their thoughts, but a tendency to run into blank spells. They say that they are not having any thoughts. This brings us to another important aspect of psychoanalytic treatment. The patient's flow of thoughts tends to be interrupted from time to time by some internal resistance within the patient.

A. B. ◆ Does this happen often, or at a certain point in the treatment?

Dr. Hammett ◆ It happens whenever something is coming up in the patient's mind that is difficult for him to deal with, or which was difficult when he initially experienced it, maybe when he was five or six years old. He may be on the verge of

12

having a memory, a painful memory, something that happened that he really couldn't deal with when it happened. As that memory begins to become almost conscious, he will probably resist the memory.

A. B. ✦ How do you handle that?

Dr. Hammett ✦ We're alert. We detect these hesitations and halts in the flow of thoughts. When they occur, if the patient isn't aware of it himself (though he usually is), we call his attention to it. Then we try to get him to find out what is causing him to block, or hesitate, or resist his thought. Is he embarrassed, is he afraid we'll think him silly, is he afraid that we'll make a moral judgment against him and think that he's bad, or something of that sort?

A. B. ✦ Can you usually overcome this resistance right away?

Dr. Hammett ✦ Minor resistances can usually be overcome within a matter of minutes. Major resistances may go on for a number of sessions, but this will be when some of the really crucial and most difficult part of the illness is about to come to the surface.

A. B. ✦ Can you think of a patient who came to this crucial moment?

Dr. Hammett ✦ One had the memory of an angry, bitter quarrel with his father; storming away up the stairs, the patient thought "I wish you would drop dead!" That night the father died of a heart attack. When that memory just about came into consciousness during a session, it met resistance and he blocked for a while.

A. B. ✦ That *would* be a resistant memory.

While the patient is lying on the couch, you're probably taking notes.

Dr. Hammett ✦ I don't take any notes during the session.

A. B. ✦ Do you interrupt the patient a lot?

Dr. Hammett ✦ More or less, depending upon the content. This varies from analyst to analyst. The only way I know this is from what patients tell me who have been to other analysts.

I gather that some analysts say very little, while others are much more active.

A. B. ✦ How long does this treatment take?

Dr. Hammett ✦ It's a long treatment. Psychoanalysis is rarely consummated quickly. So that I would say anywhere from about two years upwards to several years.

A. B. ✦ How do you know when the end is in view?

Dr. Hammett ✦ By improvement in the feeling of well-being, diminishment of the distress that caused one to seek treatment initially, and the disappearance of symptoms.

A. B. ✦ You hear a lot of stories about patients who are very attached to their analyst and don't want to let go. How do you handle this transference?

Dr. Hammett ✦ In analysis we take any feeling that the patient has about us as being not determined by our actual personality and who we actually are, but as being something that the patient felt earlier in life for some other important person, as for example, toward the father or the mother, or a brother or a sister, which he is transferring to us in the treatment context. Now if he sat up and faced us and talked to us that way, we would be very real individuals to him, and he would probably react to us to a considerable extent in terms of what we really are.

A. B. ✦ Would that be helpful?

Dr. Hammett ✦ Not in doing analysis, because in analysis we are trying to help the patient find out what happened earlier in his life, perhaps with his father or mother or both, that is still affecting him and making him sick. So that when we sit out of sight of him, we become a rather nonexistent, somewhat unreal person, and what then comes into his mind are fantasies and memories from the past which he displaces onto us, or transfers onto us without realizing that it comes from his past. A typical example of this would be a male patient who might have had an inordinate fear of his father and his father's discipline and anger. He might well develop an unrealistic fear

of the analyst with the idea that the analyst was very
disapproving, harsh, and so on.

A. B. ✦ You mean because you're so quiet and out of sight, he
must be making all this up in his mind?

Dr. Hammett ✦ That's right. It's coming up in his mind from the
past and he is transferring it to us because we are the only
other person there.

A. B. ✦ Do you find that most people in free association go back
to the early years, or do they spend a lot of time in talking
about the here and now?

Dr. Hammett ✦ More of the latter. The connections with the
early years gradually come, usually with a little help from the
analyst, who may say, "When did you have that feeling
before? Can you remember?" And often enough the patient
will, after a moment's hesitation, recall an incident from his
earlier life.

A. B. ✦ Psychoanalysis is based on the oedipal conflict, sort of a
turning point in developmental history. What exactly is that?

Dr. Hammett ✦ All children from roughly four to six normally
develop a very strong interest in the parent of the opposite
sex, the daughter toward the father and the son toward the
mother. This is a childlike version of what we would call, in
an adolescent, infatuation. It usually takes the form of being
enamored and wanting to have intimate physical contact. Of
course, at the age of four and a half, a boy doesn't really know
what sexual intercourse is nor does a girl. And yet if you
watch children, you'll see that they at least know what part of
the body is most concerned in this, because they will, if
permitted, hug and embrace and rub against the parents, and
so on.

A. B. ✦ Well, then, how does this go wrong if the mother and
father are loving . . .?

Dr. Hammett ✦ It goes wrong in one of two ways. One is for the
parents to be too responsive. In other words, if the father
whose little daughter is having her oedipal crush on him likes

it too much, and holds her on his lap too much and caresses her too much or even takes her into bed with him, it is apt to overstimulate her, and she will have difficulty growing through this stage. This does happen.

A. B. ♦ One always thinks of the parents who are too cruel.

Dr. Hammett ♦ That's the other thing that can go wrong. If the parents are completely intolerant of the child's behavior at this stage, if it makes them so anxious that they can't tolerate it and they're cruelly prohibitive, then it's difficult for the child to grow through the stage.

A. B. ♦ It would seem almost impossible to strike this delicate balance.

Dr. Hammett ♦ A lot of parents manage it. I can't give you percentages, but I guess I would say that the majority of parents manage to find the balance.

A. B. ♦ If the child gets hung up at that stage, what does that mean? He or she is not then able to have a satisfactory relationship later because he still wants the parent?

Dr. Hammett ♦ That will be in all probability the consequence. If the child gets hung up, he will do the only thing that is available to him, which is to repress it all, push it down out of consciousness. Once placed there, it will live forever; it won't die. Then at the age of twenty-one or twenty-two, this person will still be unconsciously seeking the old relationship. This will produce an internal conflict and will impair more mature development.

A. B. ♦ Is that the first point at which the neurosis begins to show most strongly, after the adolescent developmental years are over?

Dr. Hammett ♦ Yes, that's when the symptoms are likely to appear. In analyzing patients we often find that during childhood there was a brief neurosis of perhaps a few weeks' duration or a few months', during which time symptoms similar to the ones which break out in adulthood occurred. But, ordinarily, it is in early adult life that the symptoms appear.

A. B. ◆ What do you consider the best age for psychoanalysis?

Dr. Hammett ◆ Anywhere from twenty to forty.

A. B. ◆ And after forty?

Dr. Hammett ◆ I think it's still possible. When I studied psycho-analysis I was taught that it was very difficult to do analysis with a person past forty . . .

A. B. ◆ People were too rigid?

Dr. Hammett ◆ . . . that their characters and their ways of thinking and feeling were too set by that time. I do not agree with this. I think that some very good results can be achieved with persons past this age. It's harder, though.

A. B. ◆ The little ruts in their mind are all worn in.

Dr. Hammett ◆ The layers of repression, the layers of habitual use of defense mechanisms have become so thick. They are only so thick at the age of twenty-two, but by the time one is forty-two, they are twenty years thicker, from years of repeated use.

A. B. ◆ That's a good way of putting it. If I came to you as a patient, and I said to you, "I have a fear of flying, with physiological symptoms, which *I conquer* by just flying, taking various kinds of pills to do it, and also I even took flying lessons in a small plane in order to conquer it, but *didn't* succeed"—how would you try to help me?

Dr. Hammett ◆ First of all, just let me ask you, your fear of flying is flying in the active or the passive sense? Flying the plane as a pilot, or as a passenger in a plane?

A. B. ◆ Of being a passenger in a plane, in a big commercial plane.

Dr. Hammett ◆ I would talk with you and try to determine how much this symptom bothers you. If it is giving you enough difficulty that you really have to do something about it, then I think I'd say to you that there is more than one way that you can cope with this. If you just want to get rid of this symptom as quickly as possible, you may accomplish that by behavior therapy. I would also say that if you would like to get the root cause out of your mind, so that it will never bother you again and also not cause another symptom, I would recommend analysis as the method of treatment. While we're on the subject of getting rid of symptoms, I would say this: analysis doesn't pose as a method of treatment that is better than any other for simply getting rid of symptoms.

A. B. ✦ It does not?

Dr. Hammett ✦ No. There are other methods of treatment which will rid a person of symptoms as effectively as analysis. Analysis rests its usefulness not upon just getting free of the symptoms, but upon the other things that come from analysis which are valuable.

A. B. ✦ Such as . . .

Dr. Hammett ✦ Well, I notice that patients as they progress through analysis begin to show general improvement in almost all the facets of their life activities. If they work, they begin to do better at their work, and they begin to get along better with other people in the office. They begin to report that somehow things at home are better, that they find that they love their wives more than they did; perhaps there is an improvement in their more intimate relationships, in their sexual relationships. They experience a general improvement in their social relationships and they feel easier with people.

A. B. ✦ Sounds beautiful. Sounds like a whole emergence of a human personality.

Dr. Hammett ✦ It is quite impressive to see when it occurs, and it does occur. However, I definitely do not mean to promise some kind of Shangri-La of existence, because life is never that. We can, hopefully, free people of their sick inhibitions and handicaps and help them to be more what they have the potential to be, but we can't make them perfect. One of the difficulties in doing psychoanalysis is that you have to cope with the patient's fantasy that he is going to be almost perfect when his treatment is finished, a sort of superman. He's not.

A. B. ✦ How does it work, in terms of marriage and divorce?

Do you find that when people go through analysis they are more inclined to face their situation more realistically, or that they go out in the world and find a person who more closely resembles the fantasy?

Dr. Hammett ◆ There are so many factors that come into that. There is the question of how healthy or how sick the marriage was to begin with. If one spouse becomes more healthy through treatment, the other may also benefit because the neurotic interaction lessens. In my experience analysis rarely leads to divorce, but, of course, it can happen.

A. B. ◆ How do you feel about psychoanalysis as a method of treatment?

Dr. Hammett ◆ I think that psychoanalytic theory is a tremendous contribution to our understanding of human nature, what makes it tick, what makes it get out of order, and I think that as a method of treatment, psychoanalysis is quite effective in *selected* cases. I think that it has certain disadvantages which should be openly admitted or spoken of.

A. B. ◆ What are they?

Dr. Hammett ◆ Well, it does take a long time.

A. B. ◆ And it's expensive.

Dr. Hammett ◆ And it's expensive. It takes a lot of time, a lot of effort to go to the doctor's office several times a week, and it is expensive. This means, unfortunately, that it simply isn't available to individuals who can't afford it, except that in all the large cities there are psychoanalytic clinics for persons of less means.

A. B. ◆ What is the rate of private fees these days by the hour?

Dr. Hammett ◆ Twenty-five to fifty dollars an hour, depending upon the experience and reputation of the analyst. Also, fees vary from one city to another.

A. B. ◆ If psychoanalysis has disadvantages, then what treatment using this theory would be helpful?

Dr. Hammett ◆ What we call psychoanalytically oriented psychotherapy, in which we deliberately try to keep the development of transference to a minimum. We don't encourage the patient just to free-associate all the time. We try to guide the conversation to some extent, to keep it more to the point of what seems to be related to the difficulty. This is a reasonably effective method of treatment that doesn't take as long as full-dress psychoanalysis.

A. B. ✦ How would you know what kind of an analyst you were going to find?

Dr. Hammett ✦ It's really a difficult problem for people to know how to choose a doctor or a psychiatrist, or a psychoanalyst. I think there are several places that they can get help. They can talk with friends who've had experience and see what they have to say. They can seek opportunities to talk to physicians and psychiatrists to ask them for recommendations about psychoanalysts. And, since most psychoanalytic associations have a central office, they can ask for recommendations there. Generally speaking, membership in the American Psychoanalytic Association is equivalent to certification in the other medical specialties. So that's one basic criterion—determine whether or not the analyst is a member.

I think that psychoanalysis is, more than anything else, a way to find out about yourself. Not just a way to get rid of a symptom; there are other ways of getting rid of a symptom. If one is seeking increased self-knowledge and understanding, greater awareness, greater perceptiveness and sensitivity, then psychoanalysis more than any other procedure is the method of choice.

2

Jungian
Therapy

David Hart, Ph.D.

David Hart, Ph.D.

studied Jungian analysis at the C. G. Jung Institute in Zürich, Switzerland, and at the same time studied psychology at the University of Zürich, from which he received a Ph.D. magna cum laude in 1955.

He spent four years in the armed forces during World War II, and was a first lieutenant in the Army Air Corps as a communications officer for a fighter squadron.

He has been a practicing Jungian analyst since 1956, is a member of the International Association for Analytical Psychology, and is a training analyst with the New York Institute of the C. G. Jung Foundation.

Dr. Hart's special interest is exploring the psychological and spiritual significance of fairy tales, believing that they have a unique meaning for man's fantasy life.

Adelaide Bry ✦ Dr. Hart, you are a Jungian therapist. What does that mean?

Dr. Hart ✦ A Jungian analyst or therapist is sometimes called an analytical psychologist. It means someone who has been trained in Jungian psychology in one of the several institutes. I was trained in Zürich, Switzerland, and am accepted and accredited as an analyst by the International Association for Analytical Psychology.

A. B. ✦ What does this training consist of?

Dr. Hart ✦ The heart of the training is the training analysis, which takes several years.

A. B. ✦ Several years?

Dr. Hart ✦ Yes. That means going through the process of analysis and then using it. And beyond is the control analysis, of course, which all the schools probably use, working under supervision with your first patients. Beyond that, of course, there is a good deal of theoretical study, and I had both preliminary and final examinations and a thesis.

A. B. ✦ What precisely is the theory of Carl Jung that one follows to become a Jungian therapist?

Dr. Hart ✦ It's both a theory and a practice, which one applies to one's own life. The core is respect for the unconscious life, learning how to deal with the unconscious constructively, making it conscious, to shape one's own life and grow as a person.

A. B. ✦ In other words, if you help me become aware of my unconscious processes, then intellectually I'm able to change myself and to behave differently?

Dr. Hart ✦ Yes, but it's more than intellectual. As you become aware of your unconscious processes you realize that these processes *themselves* are striving for awareness. As you help this process you gain energies which were denied to you before from the unconscious, so that the cooperation of conscious and unconscious life leads to a greater unity and greater strength within the individual. Instead of working against yourself you begin to work for yourself.

A. B. ⬧ Just the releasing of this unconscious material helps to release energy?

Dr. Hart ⬧ Yes. First, as one proceeds one finds that in Jung's view there is a sort of goal-directedness. The psyche tends towards a future goal of development, which Jung calls "the self." The self embodies both conscious and unconscious personalities and gives an overall unity to the person. It's confirmed as you go on working in analysis that indeed the goal toward which you may have been striving unconsciously becomes more and more realized as you reconcile yourself to and become more aware of more and more parts—the split-off parts of your personality.

A. B. ⬧ The self in other words is going towards a goal. The self is *always* striving whether or not you have the Jungian therapy, but this therapy helps you to realize this. Is that correct?

Dr. Hart ⬧ Yes. Many so-called symptoms that are regarded in Freudian psychology as pathological turn out to be attempts of the psyche to a greater realization . . .

A. B. ⬧ Give me an example.

Dr. Hart ⬧ If a person is working at a job which is not really up to his potential, he may feel plagued by all kinds of disturbing symptoms. He may be full of anxiety, or he may have various fears of irrational hatred. Often if you analyze what is going on, the man may really be trying to repress tendencies towards greater realization of his personality, which might lead him into a different kind of life, or to different activities, or even different relationships. In other words, for the development of his personality he might need to expand beyond the narrow life which he is now leading which, of course, produces a lot of fear, but the underlying pattern is towards realization of his potential. It makes all the difference whether one sees all his symptoms in terms of *pathology* or in terms of a *need for growth.*

A. B. ◆ In other words, it might not always be pathological if a man suddenly throws up his hands one day and says, "I'm going to quit this job and go on to something else."

Dr. Hart ◆ Absolutely. In fact, around the middle of life—Jung regards that time as very important and finds it crucial in the development of personality—one has in a sense reached a zenith of development and realized one's powers in the world, and there often comes a point where a loss of energy may occur as various symptoms. This is apparently the challenge of the unrealized personality to become realized and may, if it's faithfully followed, lead a person to an entirely different way of life, which in the largest view Jung calls preparation for death. He feels that the course of the psyche in life can be compared to the course of the sun which rises, reaches its zenith and then slowly descends.

A. B. ◆ What is this middle part of life chronologically?

Dr. Hart ◆ He says it's from the late thirties to the fifties. Of course, as the person resists change, then the time of change may be later in life and there may be a breakdown because there's been so much resistance. The more cooperation there is with this development of self the more favorable the outcome.

A. B. ◆ Is Jung talking about people who have achieved their life goals? What about people who haven't necessarily achieved this?

Dr. Hart ◆ His assumption doesn't apply to all of us. We don't all achieve our goals by middle life—but middle life is still a transition.

A. B. ◆ Would you say that Jungian therapy is best suited for any particular kind of problem? Any particular age?

Dr. Hart ✦ No, I don't think what I said about the middle half of life restricts Jungian therapy as regards age at all. I find that there are times of life such as the late teens and early twenties and sometimes around the thirties which are very critical times in many people's lives, so that what Jung calls this individuation process, which wants to develop and to unify the personality, may really be a critical question at almost *any* point of life. In the teens some of the largest questions of life are demanded of the person. That's when young people go through the greatest philosophical as well as psychological agonies. Here Jungian psychology can also offer a great deal since it leads people deeper than many other forms in the way of trying to understand basic patterns of human life.

A. B. ✦ Carl Jung sounds religious.

Dr. Hart ✦ Jung was the son of a minister. He was born in Basel, Switzerland, and grew up there. He was a medical graduate and didn't turn to psychiatry until almost the end of his medical study, when he suddenly realized it would offer him a way to combine several interests—his scientific and his archaeological interests for one thing. He was always interested in the depth of things, and it seemed to him that psychiatry would offer the way to explore the depths of human personality. He became, in fact, a sort of archaeologist of the soul, an archaeologist of the psyche.

A. B. ✦ That's a nice way of putting it. Then he became associated with Freud?

Dr. Hart ✦ Yes. He was associated with Freud for several years and in a very fruitful way. They basically never did truly agree. The final disagreement came about because when Jung's great first work was published, *Symbols of Transformation*, Jung's view of sexuality differed from Freud's.

A. B. ✦ How does it differ?

Dr. Hart ✦ Jung saw sexual energy as only a *part* of a much larger psychic energy, which is our libido. He expanded the idea of libido from the sexual to a general psychic energy which embraces all human activity and interest and, therefore, in the first place cannot be traced back to organic sexual life as it can for Freud. So Jung was able to understand a great deal about the formation of thought, mythology, imagery, imagination, and so on, which Freud saw as merely derivatives of sexual instinct.

A. B. ✦ What is different about being a Jungian therapist, for example, rather than a Freudian therapist?

Dr. Hart ✦ *The basic* Jungian respect for the unconscious—we believe that you can work creatively by *paying attention* to the unconscious either in dreams or in fantasies. This whole attitude is quite different from that of other therapies; it has its own dangers because it can lead to too great an introversion.

A. B. ✦ Let's make this concrete; if I come to you as a patient and the only thing that I say is that I am dreadfully afraid to fly, what happens to me?

Dr. Hart ✦ We would sit face to face as we are now, and we would talk as equals. I might ask you for amplification, as Jung terms it, of the problem about flying; that is, first the history of your fear of it, and many incidents or any events that might have contributed to it. Also to amplify, to try to understand what flying means in kinds of ways that you might find through spontaneous writing. Your unconscious might offer you a clue.

A. B. ✦ You might ask me to go home and write something spontaneously and bring it back?

Dr. Hart ✦ Yes. It's possible that something might come out that you wouldn't expect out of automatic writing or drawing or painting. People use all kinds of means in order to really try to understand what's going on inside of themselves instead of just what they *think* they're afraid of. It might turn out that flying meant something different. As an example, it sometimes seems to me to have something to do with the separation between the two sides of the personality; that is, the height and the depth are far apart, and the flying symbolizes that state in a person.

A. B. ◆ Let me understand this—the height and the depth in a person . . .

Dr. Hart ◆ That is, a person is separated within himself and flying would be an expression of that separation and, therefore, would be considered dangerous—the tension between the opposites. People often have dreams of being in very high places and are terrified of falling from a very high place which seems to say that in some way they are living far above their natural space. Their thinking perhaps is too high or they place themselves in too superior a position in some way, and then on the other hand they're very far apart, away from their conscious position. They feel one part of themselves as very far away from the other part; they may feel that they are very superior on the one hand and very far above things; on the other hand, they feel very far below at the same time, and the separation and tension between these opposites is hard to stand. These are example of what flying could mean, but they wouldn't necesarily mean that in your case—it would have to be determined.

A. B. ◆ Gradually feelings related to my fear of flying would come out in our discussion. And then, just by its coming out, I would be able to resolve this fear for myself.

Dr. Hart ◆ Yes, but we might find that we were farther afield. We might find that the basic problem had nothing to do with flying. It might lead to other areas as I hinted. So it might require a detour in order to get to the problem.

A. B. ◆ So taking this problem to you would be only the very top layer of the iceberg to be used as a starting point?

Dr. Hart ◆ That often is true of a symptom which is given as the basic problem . . . you take it seriously in its own terms, but then you may often find that the underlying situation is much broader and deeper than you thought and the other person thought too.

A. B. ◆ How long does Jungian therapy take, and how many times a week would I come?

Dr. Hart ◆ Some of us make predictions better than others; I find it difficult. This isn't to say that all Jungians do. Generally, I see a person perhaps once a week and I count on a continuing therapy of at least a year, possibly longer. I am directed by the unconscious life of the person, and respect that, and I cannot honestly predict which way that will go.

A. B. ◆ Are you dealing with the unconscious life in terms of dreams, and is that primary during the therapy hour?

Dr. Hart ◆ Not necessarily. Some Jungians use dreams much more rigorously than I do, but I sometimes work without dreams entirely because I feel whatever is presented is part of the unconscious life. It can be expanded in its own terms, dreams or fantasy material.

A. B. ◆ Is it a process of free association?

Dr. Hart ◆ No, we don't generally use free association, although we find that useful sometimes—especially when one feels blocked. We usually stick to the main point, which is: you are angry, that's where it is right now, so that's what you would present—where the energy is, is where one catches the importance. That's generally Jung's view. He trusts the psychic life so that he feels wherever the intensity is greatest, that's where the attention is demanded. As in a physical situation, if you have a wound or if you have a hurt somewhere, that's where the attention is needed, and it's the same in the psychic life, that you should pay attention to where the greatest hurt or anger—in other words, the greatest emotional intensity— is concentrated. There's good reason why it's there. One of the great problems is that it's being covered up by something else, and then one has to try to get a more honest statement of what's really bothering a person.

A. B. ◆ I tell you that I'm angry. Then what?

Dr. Hart ◆ You're telling *me* you're angry, and then you're hearing *yourself* tell it because I'm listening to you; you have a chance to hear yourself. Then you may hear things that you hadn't expected, because if I'm not involved and I'm still letting you be angry, it helps you to get an objective picture yourself which you might not have if you were totally absorbed in it. Also, I encourage you to express this anger in some other way . . .

A. B. ✦ Such as . . .

Dr. Hart ✦ Possibly in a fantasy, or in a drawing.

A. B. ✦ What do you mean by fantasy?

Dr. Hart ✦ Some people have an extraordinary knack for getting a picture of their whole stiuation just by relaxing and letting a picture come to their minds. It gives an accurate clue as to where they are, what the psychic situation really is.

A. B. ✦ I don't understand.

Dr. Hart ✦ They just sort of let their minds go blank, lie down and then watch what comes to their minds. They see a whole scene as we all do in imagination.

A. B. ✦ Like visualizing a picture.

Dr. Hart ✦ When they watch it *carefully*, they see a picture of what the situation is, perhaps showing them in a conflict with their parents. A whole scene will come into the mind and go on like a movie. An older person may go back to his teens where he was in conflict and it may still be there within him.

A. B. ✦ Suppose the patient recognizes this old conflict is still alive?

Dr. Hart ✦ That is pursued consciously. The person goes more deeply into his feelings about his relationships with his parents, which he couldn't do at the time. He has to go through it now. He has to admit how the situation *really* was, how he really felt about it.

A. B. ✦ He has to be honest and real about his true feelings about his parents, whatever they may have been?

Dr. Hart ✦ Yes.

A. B. ✦ When he comes to that recognition, how long would this have taken in terms of therapy?

Dr. Hart • That's hard to say. Sometimes a problem like this may be just at the point where one can realize it, and may take only a few sessions. I've had people come only three or four times and a whole-life problem seems to have been resolved just in that time because they were ripe for bringing it out, and that happens through no fault of mine or anyone's. It just happened to click at that moment.

A. B. • And it wasn't necessary to go deeply into one's whole life?

Dr. Hart • No, in some cases it isn't. A release can change a way of life and allow it to develop.

A. B. • This release came about through talking it out?

Dr. Hart • Yes. Through the development of a certain attitude of freedom about the past where they had felt bound before—now they feel free. And now they can also admit *where* they were bound and *how* they acted wrongly. It's a great mystery to me how this release comes.

A. B. • That's what I was just going to ask you.

Dr. Hart • One can't *make* it happen. People come to me and it happens quickly, or I work with people for years perhaps, and then it begins to happen more slowly.

A. B. • But there are no scientific and precise answers as to why, as to what the button is that's been pushed?

Dr. Hart • I don't know of any. This is the great mystery.

A. B. • Besides fantasy, you ask people to draw things?

Dr. Hart • Yes, sometimes. Or, they write spontaneously. This is very useful because Jung regards the personality as made up of quite a number of other personalities. He feels that there are conflcting personalities within one person, and the more one knows about the others in oneself, the better off one is. So, if you let yourself write spontaneously, you might find someone else doing the writing and you may find someone you could listen and talk to. It may be very important to realize that you have another point of view in you that's not being expressed. Someone in you wants to say it differently.

A. B. ◆ Is one of the basic theories of Jungian therapy that just the release of this material is somehow going to make you feel better?

Dr. Hart ◆ It helps. Not only the release, but the attitude which allows the release, the attitude which can finally admit other points of view, and the admission is that the ego is not in sole control of the psyche. As Jung said, "One is not master in his own house," and it's important to realize that there are many forces working within the personality that need respect.

A. B. ◆ Is there any attempt at a specific continuity from session to session?

Dr. Hart ◆ I attend to continuity sometimes when I feel it's really being avoided. At other times, if I feel that one is really following the psychic force, I let it happen because I feel that can be trusted.

A. B. ◆ How can you tell?

Dr. Hart ◆ You feel your way. There are times when I feel that some talk is an evasion, that it is superficial. Then I try to bring it back to where it was or to where I think it should be. That's a very subtle question because sometimes one has to find detours before getting back to the main point. It's very delicate, and I realize that a lot of time is often wasted in allowing all kinds of ramblings to come out because you may have to get rid of superficial problems before the real ones. That's a matter of overcoming resistance, which is very tight and hard and may need a long development of trust in the relationship with the patient.

A. B. ◆ Is there transference in the Jungian therapy relationship?

Dr. Hart ◆ Definitely yes.

A. B. ◆ Is there a discussion and analysis of the transference?

Dr. Hart ◆ Yes. Transference is very important. It's the basis for the trust which allows changes in personality. I think it's fundamental to *any* good therapy. Some Jungians don't give it much credit, but I certainly do.

A. B. ✦ How you do differ from the classical Freudians? You believe in transference and you do analyze dreams.

Dr. Hart ✦ I think the main difference is in the *attitude toward the material and toward the person rather than the work we actually do.* For instance, the fact that we regard the person and his processes as striving for wholeness, that we take it for granted that the person *himself* is striving to be well, that something within him—unconsciously—is striving in that direction.

A. B. ✦ How about homosexuals and alcoholics?

Dr. Hart ✦ I've had several. I've had a lot of homosexuals, both male and female, and a few alcoholics. In the case of alcoholics, I have found real success where the person himself was at a point where he was ready to make a real change, and not so much success at another point. So there again it wasn't something I could do by myself. I felt that the person came to me ready . . . he was an alcoholic of very long standing but he came to me apparently at a time of life where he *would* cooperate, where we could cooperate together and understand each other. So our therapy had a decisive effect, but again that's a mystery. As for homosexuals, I don't have the usual Freudian view that they necessarily need to be cured. I like to, as far as possible, take a person at face value. If you really accept him this way, you find that there is more latitude for change than there would be otherwise.

A. B. ✦ In other words, your goal is to create the whole person, whether he is homosexual or heterosexual.

Dr. Hart ✦ Yes. I don't think it's quite so important how he looks, what kind of label you attach to him, but if he is or seems a whole person, that's much more important.

A. B. ✦ How do you define this wholeness and how do you know when the "wholeness" has occurred?

Dr. Hart ✦ This is very subjective. It appears that a person is somehow growing into autonomy of his own life, an ability to guide and regulate his own life, which is not superficial,

same kind of care for each other that one should have for *one's own* psychic life. Paying attention to one's inner feelings.

A. B. ✦ You said at the beginning that even after you've gone through Jungian therapy a person must continue to be devoted to his inner life to keep learning?

Dr. Hart ✦ That's my feeling.

A. B. ✦ Suppose I had gone through your therapy, and now I'm on my own. How would I devote this care and attention to my inner life? What would I do?

Dr. Hart ✦ You'd be listening to your own states. [You'd try to ask yourself, "How do I really feel about this situation I'm in?" or "What is really happening to me now?"] If someone were disturbing you, you'd go back and reflect on what's happening. In other words, you try to give *constant* attention, not overdoing it, but delicately keeping in touch with yourself and your reactions. That's the important core. And your reactions are expressed in your dreams, if you've missed them. Consciously, your dreams will show you what you didn't see in reality and will help you, as Jung says, compensate for your own lack of insight. If you continue this way, you find yourself more or less on the way which is right for you, the individual way. Some people need, for instance, a lot more human contact than others. Some need a lot more stimulation. We are all very different, but to know which way is right is a very big thing to learn. Becoming an individual is a lonely process because you can't rely on anybody else for this knowledge about yourself. *You can't live in sort of a symbiosis with another person and expect them to solve your problems.* This constant checking with yourself really means that you are on your own island.

A. B. ✦ How do people achieve this aloneness and togetherness in a marriage?

Dr. Hart ✦ That's very difficult, but it's also very important. I see people who are married, and I sometimes see both husband and wife for many years—and I find that through faithful analysis they begin to realize what they've been demanding of the other person is unreal, and they are demanding to be saved in some way by another person. As they really realize this, they withdraw their demands, and they feel that they can let that other person be what he or she is. I see this actually happen not just intellectually, but it means you really know you cannot put your demands on *someone else*. A wife sees, "this is the way he is, this is the way I am, we differ, but I have to be as I am, and then I have to respect the way he is." It's a giant lesson. You learn quite a different way of living. Instead of secretly or overtly demanding all the time of the other person, you really *let go*.

A. B.　•　How does the "letting go" come about?

Dr. Hart　•　It comes out of faithful attention to what's happening inside you, to what you are, what you need, how you want to express yourself. What you think you're doing and what you're really doing may be two different things and so on. That inside attention leads to a kind of centering of self-respect: To know that you are more or less what you seem to be. There's not so much conflict any more. As you really accept yourself, then you can also accept the other person for the first time.

A. B.　•　Sounds like it takes a lifetime! When do you see the last point at which the human psyche might be capable of some changes? Forty-five or fifty, or younger?

Dr. Hart　•　I'd say about the minute of death.

A. B.　•　Really?

Dr. Hart　•　Any time, yes. I work with a woman now of seventy. I have several people who are fifty or sixty. The woman who is in her seventies is undergoing enormous changes involving the structure of her life: realizing, very deeply the rigidity of her whole life and breaking it down and coming to a more humble and more forgiving attitude. This is happening through therapy.

A. B.　•　She is dropping her rigidities and being humble...

Dr. Hart ✦ She works at a lot in fantasy. She watches herself going through the motions of her life. She sees herself doing various things, dealing with certain people; she sees a devil over her right shoulder who represents someone who has always controlled her actions; now she stands up and faces that devil for the first time. She sees herself standing on a pedestal and forcing others to bow before her. The use of fantasies like this has convinced her like nothing else ever did of the style of her life. She sees her cruelty and her arrogance. She sees how she masked it by a very gentle appearance.

A. B. ✦ What would make a woman in her seventies come for therapy? Wouldn't she have to have an optimistic outlook that she was going to live long enough to enjoy the fruits of it?

Dr. Hart ✦ No, she could be just driven simply by a desire to change, and the time doesn't really matter that much.

A. B. ✦ The time doesn't matter?

Dr. Hart ✦ The time that you have left. You don't think of the time. It's more the quality of life that's important, not the quantity. That's what it seems to her. I don't get any hint that she thinks life is over. I know people much younger who feel their lives are over, who are without hope. I can't see that it depends on age. There are people in their thirties who are desperate. This woman is still in the middle of the struggle.

A. B. ✦ That's beautiful that people of any age can be treated, that they're receptive at *that* moment.

If you were to tell me the main belief of Jung's on which you base your theory and your therapy, what would it be?

Dr. Hart ✦ I guess it's respect for the whole person or for the psyche, and the wholeness which is striving to be realized. I can't think of any better approach to psychotherapy than that. It means to take a person at face value.

A. B. ✦ Face value?

Dr. Hart ✦ When a person comes to me, I try to take him as he is. This is not always the case with therapists. Some therapists say to themselves, "What does *that* really mean? What is he *really* saying? What is he *hiding*?" I take it as it comes—not always successfully. When I can do that, I offer more basis for development. If a person is taken seriously, as *he is now*, then he has additional self-respect, which he needs. Out of this he can begin to examine himself. I think you have to play it very carefully and respectfully with the way a person presents himself. If you say he's resisting and so on, that may be true, but it doesn't mean that what he is presenting is wrong. In presenting his feelings he is doing the very best he can just as he is, and this is the best that he can offer, whatever he is. The very fact that he is seeing me means that he is offering the best. He wouldn't be bothering to see a therapist if he weren't after something. I have to be very careful not to judge, if I can help it, on preconceived ideas like, she ought to be doing more, she ought to be making money, or she ought to be working or away from her parents. I can think of a lot of things like that. Every time you judge a human being this way you undercut him *where he is*. So, you have to be very careful. It may look like a hopeless situation to you, but you must not judge because your standards are not being used.

A. B. ♦ So what you strive for is complete acceptance of this human being . . .

Dr. Hart ♦ I think you strive for it; you never reach it. You never reach it.

3

Frommian Therapy

Erwin Singer, Ph.D.

Erwin Singer, Ph.D.

was born in Vienna, graduated from the gymnasium there, and attended the university until Hitler took over Austria in March, 1938.

He then emigrated to the United States, settling in New York City, where he received his B.S. at the City College of New York. After serving in the United States Army as a clinical psychologist, he received his M.A. and Ph.D. from New York University.

When he took postdoctoral training at the famed William Alanson White Institute in New York, he came under the influence of Erich Fromm, one of the Institute's founders. That influence is part of Dr. Singer's psychotherapy today.

Now Dr. Singer is a member of the faculty at that same Institute, as well as Professor of Psychology at City College, and Visiting Professor at New York University.

His thirty publications include a recently published book, Key Concepts in Psychotherapy.

Adelaide Bry ✦ Dr. Singer, what kind of psychotherapist are you?

Dr. Singer ✦ I think of myself as a psychoanalyst, in, hopefully, the *best* sense of the word—that is, concerned with the substance of the procedure rather than with its technicalities or trappings.

A. B. ✦ How do you define a psychoanalyst in 1971?

Dr. Singer ✦ I would think the same way as one defined a psychoanalyst, if there had been some, and I'm sure there were, in 1571!

A. B. ✦ Which is . . .

Dr. Singer ✦ Somebody who is interested in learning something about the inner arrangement of the person he meets and concerned with helping him to become familiar with his inner arrangement.

A. B. ✦ Then you follow the philosophy of Freud, generally.

Dr. Singer ✦ You see, I think it is to the *everlasting* credit of Freud that he concerned himself precisely with this discrepancy between what man believes about himself and what is really true about him. I think that Freud eventually got, as the young have it, "hung up," and certain generalizations that he thought were valid, are not valid.

A. B. ✦ Such as?

Dr. Singer ✦ Such as his particular understanding of instinctual forces, and oedipal strivings. But that is really secondary. That is like accusing Marx of not having been a creative thinker because he predicted that revolutions would take place first in industrial societies. And it did not turn out that way at all. But that does not detract from his developing a powerful method of historical analysis. The particular predictions on which a man gets stuck are quite secondary to the basic leitmotif of his vision.

A. B. ✦ So you follow the *primary* vision in Freud?

Dr. Singer ✦ Yes. I think that the primary vision, that our consciousness is like the tip of an iceberg . . . that is true . . . but I do *not* follow his assumptions about what is under the surface.

A. B. ✦ What theory do you follow for that part *under* the surface?

Dr. Singer ✦ I think I was enormously influenced by Erich Fromm.

A. B. ✦ Tell me something about him: what he means for you as a person.

Dr. Singer ✦ Historically, he is a man who grew up intellectually between two world wars, in Germany under the Weimar Republic, in the social, economic, and political turmoil of those days. And his keen and inquiring mind saw clearly the destructive hypocrisies and contradictions all around him. Freud also saw foibles all around him, but Fromm saw their nature in much broader, much more encompassing terms, and therefore his vision of man and man's genius for good and evil seems to me more compelling than the vision Freud advanced.

Personally, I had the good fortune of having been a student of Fromm, had the good fortune to have been supervised by him, and even though he is about twenty years older than I am, I experience myself more as a child of his time than of Freud's era. I suppose there is less of a generation gap between us than there is between Freud's thinking and mine.

A. B. ✦ What is it in Erich Fromm that you follow?

Dr. Singer ✦ I will have to use certain metaphors, and I'm using the metaphors that I'm using because of my first professional love. I was originally interested in the theater and trained for work in this area, and, I suppose fortunately, recognized that

44

I didn't have enough talent to be a really good actor or eventually a good director.

A. B. ⬩ The drama of the psyche!

Dr. Singer ⬩ Yes! As I see the fundamental conception in Fromm, it is a particular drama, a particular unavoidable dilemma that human beings encounter. Now Freud also wrote a drama. The Freudian Faust has a particular dilemma and he gets caught on the horns of this dilemma: the conflict between his instincts, essentially regressive self-destructive tendencies —somewhere little Eros gets off, but he doesn't pay a lot of attention to it—and a world remarkably inhospitable that does not allow a man to act out his basic regressive tendencies. Thus, Freud's *Civilization and Its Discontents*.

A. B. ⬩ Be more specific about where you think Freud misses for you.

Dr. Singer ⬩ I see no evidence for his continuous insistence upon man, in constant search of stimulus-avoidance, always eager to find a homeostatic state, and his viewing all of man's achievements—limited and dangerous as some may be—as remarkable sublimations of essentially regressive strivings. I see neither clinical nor experimental evidence for this position.

Frommian man is confronted, I believe, by *different* dilemmas.

A. B. ⬩ What dilemmas?

Dr. Singer ⬩ Fromm spells them out under headings unfortunately grossly overused and misused by some today. He calls them the *existential dichotomies*.

A. B. ⬩ That's a complicated phrase. What does it mean?

Dr. Singer ⬩ It merely means dilemmas which inevitably arise out of the peculiar nature of man, dilemmas which derive from our strange position in nature, from the obvious fact that we are clearly animals, yet more than animals—endowed with consciousness and reason, in the image of God, yet obviously far from godliness.

A. B. ⬩ What does Fromm say man's problem is?

Dr. Singer ✦ Man's reason makes him capable of painfully anticipating the end of his reason, his own death. Furthermore, the inherent problem is man's ability to recognize his relative insignificance, precisely because he *is* endowed with this most significant aspect of creation—reason. And this endowment with reason makes man also capable of seeing his essential aloneness. I do not mean *loneliness,* but *aloneness,* that separateness which raises within him the question "Was I really heard or understood?" since clearly no one can ever really crawl into the skin of anybody else. Most likely our central problem boils down to an inevitable, unavoidable, overburdening sense of responsibility which comes from recognizing this separateness.

A. B. ✦ A *responsibility* arises from this aloneness?

Dr. Singer ✦ A psychological recognition forces itself up on one. An awareness that while in the long run "I am an animal and subject to animal instincts, I am at the same moment more than an animal. I can fight my animal instincts if I choose to, and the question is will I fight them, or won't I fight them? Will I be Esau, who for a dish of lentils, betrays his father and himself, or, will I, despite the fact that these tendencies are strong within me, take a stand?"

A. B. ✦ So this is where Erich Fromm is . . . philosophically.

Dr. Singer ✦ As understood by me. But it's not philosophical. What makes it exciting is that this is a psychological issue, because these are moments of truth which have a universal impact.

A. B. ✦ How do you take the psychology of Fromm and translate it into a therapy which you use with a patient?

Dr. Singer ✦ There again I become a Freudian...because Freud was convinced (and this is to his everlasting credit) that there is universal validity in something psychoanalytic that was said two thousand years ago.

A. B. ✦ What was that?

Dr. Singer ✦ *You shall know the truth and the truth shall set you free.* Assume that the patient comes to my office (I don't even like to call a person a patient) . . . the *other person* comes to my office in the hope that he will be heard and that nobody will pull any punches and that some basic realistic tendencies about him will be exposed—that there will be a progressively expanding personal self-knowledge that will not necessarily make him happy but will *free* him, in the sense of reducing shame about himself.

A. B.   ✦   You're trying to uncover layers of untruth that the person has built about himself, get down to the essential of whatever this person may be.

Dr. Singer   ✦   Correct.

A. B.   ✦   What kinds of *concrete* problems do you encounter in your practice?

Dr. Singer   ✦   These "other persons" come with all kinds of concrete problems, which are, to be very frank, by and large, commonplace. Work issues, marital-love issues, physical complaints of all kinds. I consider it my responsibility to help that person see as soon as possible that the remediation of these problems is not the legitimate concern of therapy.

A. B.   ✦   That problems in his job or with his wife are not to be part of your discussion with the patient?

Dr. Singer   ✦   Absolutely. That they can only serve as points of departure. That in no way could I be concerned with helping him "solve" these problems, that it would actually be demeaning to both of us if I tried to help him or her arrange life in a more comfortable fashion.

A. B.   ✦   What then *do* you talk about after you've told the patient that you're not interested in those things?

Dr. Singer   ✦   I don't say I don't want to hear about these things, but I try to get involved in an exploration of his character, of his scheme of values, and to get at the discrepancy between the avowed values and the really maintained values. You get an awful lot of people who visit you thinking of themselves as kind or liberated or avant-garde and even some who strenuously avow socialism or some similar philosophy.

A. B. ⋆ And you are trying to help this person discover whether he really lives what he says he believes?

Dr. Singer ⋆ Yes, I try to get at that discrepancy. I'll put it plainly. If somebody were honestly a socialist and lived like a socialist and believed in a genuine socialistic existence, he wouldn't have any need to consult me. I might come to consult him.

A. B. ⋆ So the basic goal of your therapy is—See clearly the way you live and the way you pretend to live, see clearly the way you feel and pretend you feel.

Dr. Singer ⋆ We all pretend to ourselves. I think of neurosis as an attempt to keep personal pretenses going by obscuring to ourselves the true nature of our motivations, a way of having one's cake and eating it. It's so common to hear people complain about how mistreated they have been by some parent. Now, I do not doubt that they have been mistreated, but if that were all that there was to it, one might encounter a sad person and a person justifiably saddened by life's events. But this is not neurosis or psychosis, and what is a psycho-analyst to do about it other than humanly sympathize with the ill fortunes of the other person? But as one listens further and observes the patient's life and actions, it all too often becomes all too clear that despite all the protestations to the contrary he has modeled himself very much in the image of the oppressor against whom he rails and merely pretends that he is different. Neurosis is such an enormous obscuration procedure.

A. B. ⋆ What kind of patients do you see?

Dr. Singer ⋆ The same most of us see. By and large, upper-middle-class or middle-class, fairly well-educated people. But I have worked with blue-collar persons. And the interesting thing about working with them was that I could not find what one hears so much about, that there is such a tremendous difference in the *basic* concerns . . . between the upper and lower socioeconomic groups.

A. B. ◆ Can you think of a real problem you're working with now?

Dr. Singer ◆ That is tricky, but...

A. B. ◆ It's easier to understand your method that way.

Dr. Singer ◆ Let me think how I can disguise someone. I did work recently with a young man who by and large would be considered functioning well, and discharging certain professional responsibilities well . . . . But he was operating at an inordinate expense of energy, always having the gnawing sense of not accomplishing anything, and then letting his frustration out o nothers around him.

A. B. ◆ . . . You said, "an inordinate expense of energy". . . running around not accomplishing anything?

Dr. Singer ◆ Yes...winding up in total exhaustion each day at 5:00 P.M. . . . suspicious of others, annoyed with friends and family, just plain unpleasant to live with. He was "aware" of himself . . . and "in touch" or whatever the term in vogue these days is . . . with his feelings, attitudes, and desires. But as the investigation proceeded it became apparent that he was lying to others and to himself. This is the question—how could he trust others when he did not trust himself?

A. B. ◆ On what level did he not believe himself?

Dr. Singer ◆ He told himself how devoted he was to the betterment of man and to the advancement of the downtrodden; but it became quite apparent that a good deal of it was purely selfish, designed not to really *do* something but to show that he was better than someone else, and it takes quite an enormous amount of energy to do anything while constantly being involved with upstaging someone else. It becomes a double task, and even a triple task, to keep that knowledge from oneself.

A. B. ◆ Sounds exhausting. How do you treat something like that? . . . Sounds like you have to cut away at the roots of his character.

Dr. Singer ✦ Here again I become a Freudian, since it was Freud who pointed out that the here and now, the interaction, the transaction between the two people in the office, and how the patient reacts, is all important. And the reactions he calls forth in me will hopefully expose, among other things, his intense competitive feelings in relation to me . . . while he tells himself so frequently that he is concerned with my welfare.

A. B. ✦ Can you think of a conversation you had with this man which shows precisely what you are talking about?

Dr. Singer ✦ One day, when I had been quite ill and returned to work prematurely, he kept on expanding on one of his supposedly very considerate actions and how they went unrewarded while I was growing progressively sicker. I finally told him that I could not go on with our session, that I was feeling ill again, but I managed to mention before he left (he was somewhat annoyed about the interruption) that it seemed strange to me that a man of his vision and concern wouldn't have noticed how ill I looked and acted. When we met again the conversation turned again to this episode and fortunately it was possible for him to recapture his essential disinterest in the other person's—in this instance in my own— welfare. This was quite disturbing to him, but at least it allowed for profitable exploration of the pretense of his concerns, its historical roots, and its usefulness in his life.

A. B. ✦ That is typical dialogue? Is it mostly like that, two people sitting in comfortable chairs looking at each other?

Dr. Singer ✦ Yes, I prefer it this way most of the time. Some people like to lie down on the couch, and that is why I have it. I suspect there are times when it is appropriate for the person to use the couch in order to be able to concentrate more pointedly. Not so that I become mysterious, but I too sometimes find it quite useful myself to stare at a blank ceiling. To find a setting of minimum destraction from my thoughts, my inner sense . . . the ceiling can be useful.

A. B. ✦ You mean the patient can choose the chair or the couch when he enters the office each hour?

Dr. Singer ⬩ Yes, of course, it makes little difference to me. But I do like to know why a person changes from one preferred mode to another.

A. B. ⬩ When you are in dialogue and you are both in chairs, that's a more involved relationship, isn't it?

Dr. Singer ⬩ I hope so, but it is difficult. The young people talk about involvement in easy terms as though it were duck soup. Maybe they find being involved easy. To me it seems a difficult undertaking.

A. B. ⬩ How do *you* feel about the patient, the person ... whatever you want to call him?

Dr. Singer ⬩ Some people talk about *them* as the other participant, some people refer to the therapist as a participant observer. Fromm once said that it might be better said the other way around, an *observing participant*. Either one makes sense.

A. B. ⬩ Now you're still talking with him about the discrepancy in his lifestyle and his feelings ...

Dr. Singer ⬩ As it shows in his relationship to me. Because what a man usually tells me is like yesterday's newspaper: it's stale. But when he talks of his beautiful soul, and then barely notices that I have apparently become rather ill during the hour, there is some fascinating discrepancy here.

A. B. ⬩ He's not seeing you at all.

Dr. Singer ⬩ Like so many people, he loves humanity but to care for individuals is a far different story.

A. B. ⬩ How do you handle this in the therapy?

Dr. Singer ⬩ I'll look right at him and say, "How does this not noticing such an obvious thing, my being ill, go with your beautiful soul?"

A. B. ⬩ And then?

Dr. Singer ⬩ Hopefully he will think about this and capture the knowledge of his own self-absorption, his own self-preoccupation, in a broader sense than Freud's, his narcissism.

But that's just a dirty word.

A. B. ✦ A dirty word?

Dr. Singer ✦ It doesn't tell the complete sense of sham, the experience of the moment, the sense "I don't give a damn for the other person."

A. B. ✦ To penetrate that sham . . .

Dr. Singer ✦ Oh . . . he was very preoccupied with appearance. Not physical appearance, but the impression he makes on those whom he actually values or would like to impress for whatever reasons, and therefore feels compelled to impress with fancy stories . . . and then he starts to believe in them himself.

A. B. ✦ How did you finally get this person to change?

Dr. Singer ✦ I did not "get him to change." That is his job. But through persistent confrontations of this order and through painstaking exploration of his feelings and associations he came to a point of self-recognition which made meaningful choice possible, reduced the driven quality of his behavior and living. With the growing clarity of his situation and inner life, obscuration became less and less necessary.

A. B. ✦ How long does it take to get a person to come to grips with this essential psychological recognition, to throw away the sham, and see his essential being?

Dr. Singer ✦ I can answer that with a cliché, but it's true, like some clichés: a lifetime. That doesn't mean a lifetime with me or any therapist. . . . For anything fruitful to come from psychoanalysis the person must walk out of here with both of us convinced that he will continue searching himself for the rest of his life. Then I feel I've earned my money.

A. B. ✦ You've put him on a mental path, a *way* of looking.

Dr. Singer ✦ I have not—he has. And he may make choices which I don't like. But how he uses what he finds out is really none of my business, all I can do is to be hopeful that his way will lead to a continuous search throughout his life.

A. B. ✦ Your therapy, then, is to help one human being to see himself in relationship to the world, in a very big way, and a little way, all at the same time.

Do you see your patients with frequency . . . once, twice, or even more each week?

Dr. Singer ✦ I prefer to see a person as frequently as possible, as much as both of us (myself and the patient) can stand.

A. B. ✦ Why?

Dr. Singer ✦ Because I believe this kind of self-investigation is under the best of circumstances a very, very difficult task. And the circumstances are never the best. So the sense of continuity, the possibility of picking up tomorrow, or at least the day after tomorrow, where one was, to catch something in the air, the theme that was there, that seems terribly important. There are so damn many diversions, diversions that both analyst and patient like to engage in, that I prefer at least three times each week.

A. B. ✦ And how long does your therapy last? In your hands?

Dr. Singer ✦ In *my* hands?

A. B. ✦ In the *other's* hands.

Dr. Singer ✦ That is right. That is exactly what I mean. I think there are enormous individual differences. I remember working with a woman for a year and a half—a checker in a supermarket—with what I thought were remarkable results.

A. B. ✦ Why were they remarkable?

Dr. Singer ✦ Because this woman had a real talent to get to the heart of herself, and therefore managed in a relatively short time to face herself, and that made it possible for her to dispense with fooling herself through symptoms—physical ones I mean—in a relatively short order.

A. B. ✦ Did you find working with someone like this different from your usual kind of patient?

Dr. Singer ✦ Very. You can't hide behind words with relatively unsophisticated people. It's not that they are more difficult to *help;* they are difficult to *stand* because they really put one to the test all the time. Fancy words mean nothing. With them I have to think ... What do I really mean? Is this a newspaper filler or a fancy headline?

A. B. ✦ You're saying that your middle-class and upper-middle-class patients are so clever with words that even the therapist is drawn into the verbal game?

Dr. Singer ✦ I think the therapist often starts it. But I feel the educated patient eventually catches on quickly to a lot of word-fencing and nonsense. The therapist can say, "All right, you want to hide and amuse yourself with cleverness, I'll give you a half hour for that."

A. B. ✦ Do you spend a lot of time in your therapy on early childhood, or do you deal more with here and now?

Dr. Singer ✦ I like to think that we spend time with both. Usually I do not immediately take a detailed history, and I'm not overly interested in the literal recall of childhood experiences, but more in the emotional experience, the mood, and the circumstances under which these moods arose, and the details of that mood.

A. B. ✦ And you feel that talking out plus the interaction between patient and therapist is the change agent ...

Dr. Singer ✦ I think the change has to do with a genuine capturing. One of my teachers, Clara Thompson, always used to talk about the fact that the trouble with our patients is that they have never learned that time marches on and that the emotional reactive patterns of yesterday, while realistic then, are not appropriate now. It's not an intellectual mission. I don't want to become mystical about it, but there must develop in the patient some kind of profound grasp ... like, My God, this is 1971, not 1941.

A. B. ✦ How do you think that grasp takes place?

Dr. Singer ✦ I'm not sure ... I suspect that it has something to do with the therapist's willingness to constantly reexamine himself, what he believes, and by what standards he lives. I have a notion that this willingness on the part of the therapist to face himself and to change creates a climate in which the patient starts to feel free to grasp his own emotional life. Incidentally, Fromm's intellectual and theoretical development itself is an ample illustration of this possibility of profound change. Here is a man trained in Germany in orthodox psychoanalytic theory and practice, working hard in an area attacked by all kinds of unsavory detractors, but he is willing to re-examine his position, and he dared to reformulate and significantly modify the Freudian theory in which he was trained.

A. B. ✦ How did he modify it?

Dr. Singer ✦ I'll have to say it as I understand it.

A. B. ✦ Fair enough.

Dr. Singer ✦ I think the key to the modifications he advanced is somewhere in his book *The Sane Society* and also in a later book, *The Heart of Man*. There, it seems to me, he proposes something like a single instinct theory: namely, that there is one thing that man cannot tolerate, and that is the perpetuation of the *status quo* in himself and around himself, that man is imperiously driven to transcend himself. But of course, there are only two ways to do this—by construction and by destruction. I'm more or less quoting, but to him those two, construction and destruction, rather than being two different instinctual tendencies, are just opposite sides of the same coin.

A. B. ✦ Are you saying that if a man doesn't grow, he'll turn around and destroy himself?

Dr. Singer ✦ He'll destroy either himself, somebody else, or both.

A. B. ✦ How do you apply the Frommian theory of psychological recognition to your own life?

Dr. Singer ✦ You know it has often been said that the most depressed group of people in the world are psychiatrists and psychoanalysts. I think this is a correct observation and stems from a good reason.

A. B. ✦ What's the reason?

Dr. Singer ✦ Because if one daily deals with the discrepancies and hypocrisies in the lives of others, and if you have some shred of integrity left, the discrepancies in your own life will strike you, and so I tend to be depressed about myself. But I suspect that part of my basic commitment to education and to teaching for the past twenty-five years (at City College, New York City) is an effort to overcome the source of my depression. My work as both a teacher and an analyst helps me to be an individual and yet still be a member of a community. And again, Fromm pointed that out that sanity demands one's rootedness in both oneself and a community. In the beginning of one of his books he uses the well known and ancient Jewish citation "If I'm not for myself, who will be? If I'm only for myself, who am I? If not now, when?" He sees that a basic task for man, is to be for himself and yet to be at the same time for and with others. Insanity is simply failure in this arduous task.

A. B.   •   That's perfectly said. It goes back, too, to what you said at the beginning of our conversation. The patient must recognize his insignificance but at the same time recognize his responsibility.

Dr. Singer   •   I believe my own involvement in teaching and in political activity is a reflection of an effort to solve this task. Therefore I do not try to solve the problems of the world in my office. At moments I think I can do something about them as a political person. But I'm very upset about the contemporary trend of mixing psychology and political activity in community psychiatry and community mental health programs. When one becomes a jack-of-all-trades—a bit of a lawyer, a bit of a doctor, a little bit of a clergyman, a little bit of an advisor—and tries to fulfill all these functions for hundreds of people, disaster must ensue. If I can help one person genuinely, then I think I have pulled my weight as an analyst. But it has to be meaningful help rather than some diffuse patch job.

4

Gestalt Therapy

Frederick Perls, M.D.

Frederick Perls, M.D.

lovingly called "Fritz" by his many friends, died in March, 1970, at the age of 76, about eight months after he recorded this interview. He was both a psychiatrist and a psychologist. But he was a disdainer of labels. As one of the foremost originators of Gestalt psychology, Perls founded in 1952, the Gestalt Institute in New York City, together with his wife, Laura, Paul Goodman, Elliot Shapiro, and Paul Weisz. Since then, many institutes have been formed throughout the country.

Perls saw the Gestalt in the "undistorted, natural approach to life," that is, thinking, feeling, and acting, as one.

The average person, raised in an atmosphere of splits, loses this wholeness. The word Gestalt comes from the German; there is no exact English equivalent but a close definition is "meaningful organized whole."

His widow, Mrs. Laura Perls, continues to run the New York Institute and is herself a leader in the field of Gestalt psychotherapy.

Adelaide Bry ✦ Dr. Perls, what is Gestalt therapy?

Dr. Perls ✦ Discussing, talking, explaining is unreal to me. I hate intellectualizing, don't you?

A. B. ✦ Sometimes, but I want to interview you. I want to know about Gestalt therapy. So . . .

Dr. Perls ✦ Let's try something else. You be the patient. *Be real* . . . no more intellectualizing.

A. B. ✦ Well, if it's what you want, I'll try it. I'll *try* being the patient. . . . Here's what I'd say to you then: "I'm Adelaide and I come to you, Fritz Perls, as a patient. I'm depressed and I also have this physiologically expressed fear of flying. My hands get clammy. My heart beats rapidly." Now what?

Dr. Perls ✦ I'd cure you of your physiologically expressed fear of flying in five minutes.

A. B. ✦ Oh, you would? All right. How would you do that?

Dr. Perls ✦ Close your eyes. Go into the airplane. Realize you're not in a real airplane, just in your fantasy. So fantasy is going to help you see what you experience when you are flying.

A. B. ✦ Already my heart begins to beat faster . . .

Dr. Perls ✦ Don't open your eyes . . .

A. B. ✦ All right . . .

Dr. Perls ✦ Your heart begins to beat faster . . . go on.

A. B. ✦ I see the back of the pilot up there, and you know I'm not sure whether he can do it.

Dr. Perls ✦ Good. Get up and tell him that.

A. B. ✦ I tap him on the shoulder, he looks around, I say, "Are you keeping your eyes on the road?" He shoves me away and I go back to my seat.

Dr. Perls ✦ Now you don't go back to your seat. Change seats.

You're the pilot. [Dr. Perls asked me to get up, sit in another chair facing the one I was previously sitting in. Each time I changed roles, I changed seats.]

A. B. ◆ I'm the pilot. What is this woman doing interfering with me? Get out of the cockpit and get back to your seat. *I know what I'm doing.*

Dr. Perls ◆ I don't believe your voice. Listen to your voice.

A. B. ◆ [As airplane pilot] I'm sorry, madam, I'm very sorry, madam, terribly sorry, but we do know how to run this airplane, and would you please go back to your seat. Everything is fine and under control.

Dr. Perls ◆ O.K. now. What's your name? Adelaide? Adelaide.

A. B. ◆ [As Adelaide] I'd like to go back to my seat, but I'm upset about this airplane, because I don't like to be off the ground. I don't like to be fifty thousand feet up in the air. It's not natural to me.

Dr. Perls ◆ O.K., now you are a writer—write this script.

A. B. ◆ [As pilot] Listen, we do the best we can, we're human beings, too. You know this plane is checked by Pan American and this plane cost five million dollars and believe me, if there's one thing we like it's money, and every time a plane goes down we lose money, we lose people. It's very bad for our public relations and we do everything possible to keep this plane in the air. Now, if once in a while . . . my God . . . if once in a while we slip up, that's the way it goes and you gotta take your chances on this earth. So far we've had absolutely no transatlantic accidents. Do you realize that? [As Adelaide] But, I, me, it would be just my fate going to London, you know, going to London, whup down in the middle of the Atlantic Ocean. But, you know, so what. So I'd miss old age, I'd miss a lot of horrible things, so maybe it wouldn't be so bad after all.
[As pilot] Listen, lady, that's no way to think when you're going off on a holiday. You're being absolutely stupid.

Dr. Perls ◆ Say this again.

A. B. ◆ [As pilot] You're being absolutely stupid, stupid, stupid, stupid, stupid. What the hell. I do this for a living. Even if I'm making fifty thousand a year. I can do something else. I do this for a living. Every day—no, not every day— fifteen days a month I do this for a living and you are a stupid woman.

[As Adelaide] I already know I'm stupid. That's a joke, I know I'm stupid. You know, I have to tell you . . . I've even taken flying lessons. I took flying lessons to try to do something about the fear, *in little Piper Cubs.*

Dr. Perls ◆ Don't tell me . . .

A. B. ◆ [As pilot] Piper Cubs, oh, Piper Cubs, right. Piper Cubs, that's a joke. You're in a Boeing 707, Piper Cubs. There's no relationship between the two of them. I suggest, madam, that you go back to your seat, and that you let me . . .

Dr. Perls ◆ I suggest something else. You take over now, the plane. You go to the pilot's seat.

A. B. ◆ [As Adelaide] Ooooooooo, I love it. All I know is I love being in control.

Dr. Perls ◆ Don't tell me. This is him.

A. B. ◆ [As Adelaide] Listen, I can fly this plane better than you can with my left hand behind my back. You know there are a few little dials and technical things around here, but I could learn that in about a couple of months. You know I'm bright enough to learn that. Now you sit back there and I'm going to run this show.

Dr. Perls ◆ Say this again: "I'm going to run the show."

A. B. ◆ I'm going to run this show.

Dr. Perls ◆ Again.

A. B. ◆ I'm going to run this show.

Dr. Perls ◆ Say this with your whole body.

A. B. ◆ I'm going to run this show.

Dr. Perls ◆ Now, say this to me: "Fritz, I'm . . .

A. B. ◆ Fritz, I'm going to run this show.

Dr. Perls ◆ Again.

A. B. ♦ I'm going to run this show.

Dr. Perls ♦ Have you learned something?

A. B. ♦ Yeah, that's me—*unfortunately.*

Dr. Perls ♦ There you get a little piece of Gestalt therapy.

A. B. ♦ It's beautiful.

Dr. Perls ♦ You get an example now that *we are not analyzing.* We are just integrating. You have given the pattern. Some of your domineering needs, and I let you take it back so you feel a little bit stronger.

A. B. ♦ Right, right.

Dr. Perls ♦ That's Gestalt therapy.

A. B. ♦ I see. Does all Gestalt work this way? . . . I saw you do it yesterday in a demonstration. Do you always do it with this kind of technique, with a person changing roles and seats to emphasize a point?

Dr. Perls ♦ Whenever I see a polarity, yes. When we have two opposites. You'll notice these opposites are fighting. The passenger and the pilot, they are enemies. They are enemies because they don't listen to each other. In this dialogue, by realizing this other part, which seems to be outside of you, persecuting you, you see it is actually you, yourself. So you take those feelings back inside, you reassimilate a little of the domineering needs.

A. B. ♦ Well really, though, maybe in order for me to understand this deeply, we would have to go through it twenty times or twenty years. Or would we have to spend a year, maybe, working on this in order for it to get inside of me?

Dr. Perls ♦ No, no, no, no. Now I have to tell you what I said yesterday, that I finally found a solution. You don't need to stay twenty years on the couch or have year in, year out therapy. We can do the whole thing in about three months. From neurosis to authenticity. And the solution is the therapeutic community: where we come together, work together, and do the therapy together. The core of the therapy is learning to confront your opposites. Once you know this

way of confronting yourself with opposites, next time you
might be able to do it easier. If I give you, for instance, an
example of what is the most frequent opposite inside people,
then you'll see what will happen from this. The most frequent
opposite example is the top dog and the underdog. And we
will extrapolate from this a bit.

A. B. ✦ All right.

Dr. Perls ✦ Now. The top dog sits here [in a chair]. The top dog
starts, "Adelaide, you should . . ." [Again, I change seats as
I change roles.]

A. B. ✦ [As top dog] Adelaide, you should. You should get up
every morning at seven o'clock. Not eat too much. Exercise.
Be absolutely efficient about your writing. Get to the
typewriter at eight o'clock in the morning.

Dr. Perls ✦ Now do this stronger. . . .

A. B. ✦ [As top dog] YOU SHOULD GET TO THE
TYPEWRITER AT EIGHT IN THE MORNING.

Dr. Perls ✦ Are you aware that you are still keeping five inches
away from her?

A. B. ✦ [As top dog] Oh. I'm going to smack you down because
. . . I'm going to smack you down because you're not living
life, well, efficiently on all levels. You're too full of conflict;
you're too full of horseshit; you haven't been a good mother
to your children.

Dr. Perls ✦ O.K., change seats. *You're* the underdog.

A. B. ✦ [As underdog] I am a very needy person. I can't make
it on my own. I've got to have a man now to take care of me.
I can't stand up myself.

Dr. Perls ✦ Now, write this script.

A. B. ✦ [As underdog] He's not perfect (O.K., neither am I),
he's here and I like him very much. But if I get married, I'm
not free.

Dr. Perls ✦ Are you aware that the underdog is on the defense?

A. B. ✦ Yes.

Dr. Perls ✦ Have you noticed this? Each time you change seats, you cross legs and squeeze your genitals and even that moment you close yourself up completely.

A. B. ◆ When I become the top dog?

Dr. Perls ◆ I don't know. Right now just be aware that you're completely closed. Now talk to top dog again.

A. B. ◆ [As top dog] All right. You're a sweet little girl, but you're just not developing your potential and your conflict is because you're afraid to be an independent human being. And you've seen enough horseshit around here, you saw it in the encounter group last night [at a psychological convention in Washington, D.C.]; you perceive how goddamned afraid everybody is in terms of their ego and social relationships and you don't have that hangup. . . . You've really got it made if you only knew how to act. You don't have half the fears of all these people around here. You're about twenty levels beyond that already, and you're afraid to step into the role. Those people are just like scared little mice and you're not that at all.

Dr. Perls ◆ Do you notice that top dog is changing into pleading, persuading?

A. B. ◆ Yes. Well, I know that I probably have a lot more insight than some . . .

[As underdog] You cannot make me do what I don't want to do. You can't. You can't.

Dr. Perls ◆ You are already getting spiteful, you're on the defensive.

A. B. ◆ [As top dog] O.K. If you don't want to do it, you don't want to do it. You don't have to achieve all this goddamned horseshit you think you have to achieve; just go along and be. So, you thought one day you were going to be a good writer, and you didn't have the one thing that it takes to be the great writer, and that is the ability to sit on your ass alone eight hours a day. And if you don't have it, you don't have it. And who the hell cares. Well, it's sort of a regret, but I don't feel that regretful any more, you know. So far around it's been interesting. It's been fun. Whatever it is. . . .

Dr. Perls ✦ What do you do with your hands?

A. B. ✦ Hmmm? Equivocating? I want to use them in some way. I want to use them in some way. Maybe to, uh . . . I think I want to use them at the typewriter. I want to use them.

Dr. Perls ✦ Why?

A. B. ✦ [As underdog] Approval, you know. Love and approval. You're the big daddy and I want you to say, "Adelaide, you're great. You really are. You're really great. You're pretty goddamned good."

And, uh . . . that's all it is to be a human being on this earth. Just to be reasonable enough and have some love and some caring and survive financially. That's about what it amounts to.

Dr. Perls ✦ Change roles now!

A. B. ✦ [As top dog] But that isn't all there is, that's what you say. You've got to involve yourself in something at this point. You can't stand back anymore and just sit around. O.K. You want to involve yourself—do it. It's not such a hard thing to do. There are thousands of things going on out there. You have all kinds of ways to involve yourself. Do it and see what happens.

Dr. Perls ✦ You seem to begin to experience something.

A. B. ✦ I am. The experience is that I'm making a conflict when there really doesn't have to be one for me at this point. I'm manufacturing the conflict.

Dr. Perls ✦ I see. Well, let's see how we can solve this and go on nagging, and nudging and hear this underdog . . .

A. B. ✦ [As top dog] All right. Do it. Do it. Do it. Stand up and do it. The devil take the hindmost, you know. You've got to put the past out of your mind. Whatever happened, happened. And you've got to go on to something else. That's all. It's time to go on. It's time to go through that goddamned impasse. You've been up to it forty times. You've had a million experiences. Go through it. You know. You know more than half those people that were on stage yesterday. You understood Fritz Perls. Very well. Very well. You understood the whole thing. You wouldn't have five years ago. O.K. F—— you. F—— you. F—— you.

Dr. Perls ◆ [Underdog] How dare you say a thing like this to me?

A. B. ◆ [Underdog] How dare you say a thing like this to me? I am in charge of you. I'm gonna sit around for the next thirty years and I'm just gonna feel sorry for myself and I'm not gonna do anything. And don't you tell me what to do. Don't tell me.

I got the roles mixed up. I got mixed up.

Dr. Perls ◆ Because the roles are mixed.

A. B. ◆ That's right. I don't want to do anything. Part of this beautiful zest for life that I had, it's gone away and I keep reaching to find it again, and I can't find it. And I don't know what the spark is that would make me come alive again.

Dr. Perls ◆ Good.

A. B. ◆ I don't know. I don't give a shit about the ego. I don't know.

Dr. Perls ◆ Go back to the seat. Do it one more time.

A. B. ◆ All right. F—— you. F—— you.

Dr. Perls ◆ Put your voice in the chair. You talk to your voice.

A. B. ◆ Put my voice in that chair . . . ? My voice is beautiful. I did a radio show at one time. You are a beautiful voice. You are alive, you are interesting. It's a beautiful, low, intelligent . . . It's a voice that reflects background, and breeding. It's an excellent voice. And not only that, it's carried you very far in life. Because this kind of voice . . . when you come on with this kind of voice with people, it immediately commands something. People listen to you because it has this quality . . . [changing]

The voice is controlled . . .

Dr. Perls ◆ I am controlled.

A. B. ◆ I am controlled. I am the voice, and the voice . . .

Dr. Perls ◆ I am the voice.

A. B. ✦ Oh, I am. I am the voice, right?

Dr. Perls ✦ You be your voice.

A. B. ✦ I am controlled. I know I'm playing this role. I know I'm able to do it. I delight in it. I know what I can do with you, my voice. I know just how to use it for what I want, when I want to. No . . . ?

Dr. Perls ✦ You're not becoming your voice. I am controlling you, charming you. . . .

A. B. ✦ I'm controlling you?

Dr. Perls ✦ Charming you.

A. B. ✦ I'm charming you. I'm keeping you unreal in a way. I keep you away from the real me because I've been such a good weapon for you all your life. I've been a way of controlling your anger, you know. I've been a way of helping you get what you want at the same time. I'm good at it. I'm good at this. I really am.

Dr. Perls ✦ Let's try this. I'm the greatest manipulator. . . .

A. B. ✦ Oh. I'm the greatest manipulator on earth. But I gotta be right here. I'm the lousiest manipulator on earth because everyone sees through my manipulations after a while. In the beginning they don't, but then they see right through it. And I think I can play a game that nobody else recognizes, but they see me. They see me. And I don't realize they see me. That's the stupid part.

Dr. Perls ✦ Don't change your voice.

A. B. ✦ Woe is me. Woe is me. Woe is me. Woe is me. Woe is me. And cut out the stupidity of self-pity. Woe is me.

Dr. Perls ✦ More pity, more.

A. B. ✦ Adelaide, I feel sorry for you, but, umm. . . .

Dr. Perls ✦ Be very sorry.

A. B. ✦ I feel sorry for you and I feel sorry because God gave you a lot and you just haven't brought it all together yet. You just really haven't. You really haven't. I feel sorry for you because you can't stand up. Oh, you have stood up a lot, but you could do it more.

Dr. Perls ◆ What do you hear?

A. B. ◆ A little girl pleading.

Dr. Perls ◆ What age?

A. B. ◆ I always come to nine. There was something at nine.

Dr. Perls ◆ Again. . . .

A. B. ◆ Oh, I'm sorry for you, Adelaide, 'cause of that stupid family, and all the screaming in my ears. They ruined my ears. I couldn't listen. There was so much screaming. I couldn't listen. So I shut myself away and my ears. But it's time to open your ears now. 'Cause nobody's screaming anymore. And to hang on to your childhood is such a bore. It is such a bore. And I am so tired of thinking about it. It really doesn't interest me. If it really doesn't interest you anymore, then all you have to do is open your ears and listen. That's all there is to it. Just listen. Listen to the world. Listen to the music. And listen. Maybe that's all there is to it.

Dr. Perls ◆ Change the dialogue to your ears.

A. B. ◆ My ears. These ears are . . . my ears are closed. I am my ears and I'm all closed and I don't listen. I shut it all out. I don't want to listen. I'm hearing only one thing. I'm only hearing that terrible screaming. All that screaming. . . . All those horrible, hideous people in my family with the exception of that beautiful father. Could I listen to him? No, I couldn't listen to anybody.

Dr. Perls ◆ Your father?

A. B. ◆ He was pathetic, but nice.

Dr. Perls ◆ Talk to him.

A. B. ◆ I wish I'd loved you more when you were here. You were a sweet man, a very intelligent man, and a learned man— and I didn't listen to you. I didn't listen to you at all. I'd like to. If only my kids could listen to you. They don't have any father to listen to. Cut the self-pity. They may have something else to listen to. They have a whole different environment.

Dr. Perls ◆ What do you hear?

A. B. ◆ A mixture. I hear a mixture of him and a mixture of the screaming—both.

Dr. Perls ✦ What do you hear?

A. B. ✦ I hear the tape recorder going on and on. That's what I hear. *I got something new out of it. I heard a whole new thing that I'd never gotten, Fritz.* A credit to you and all the stuff. I got a whole thing about listening I'd never gotten before. A whole feeling about opening my ears.

Dr. Perls ✦ What do you hear?

A. B. ✦ What do I hear? *I hear myself wanting to listen.*

Dr. Perls ✦ You do not have ears yet?

A. B. ✦ I have no ears yet? I'm on the road, though, and I . . . and people are always saying to me, "But you don't listen to me. You didn't hear what I said."

Dr. Perls ✦ Shut up.

A. B. ✦ Shut up. All right. I hear him pleading with me, my father, to listen to me.

Dr. Perls ✦ What do you hear now?

A. B. ✦ Emptiness.

Dr. Perls ✦ Now. . . .

A. B. ✦ I hear the tape recorder. I hear you. Aha. Aha. I got it. I hear *what is. I hear what is now.*

Dr. Perls ✦ More. . . .

A. B. ✦ What I hear is the sound of the people in the hall. I hear you. I hear the tape recorder. I hear the air conditioner.

Dr. Perls ✦ What do you hear?

A. B. ✦ That's right. I hear what is now.

Dr. Perls ✦ You need to use your ears.

A. B. ✦ Because I got a whole new way that came over me in terms of listening. I hear myself and my voice is still out there. My voice is . . . I feel this reality inside of me which I felt for a long time. But my voice doesn't convey . . . this doesn't convey what I want to say out here. Therein lies the dichotomy.

Dr. Perls ✦ The hearing and the saying.

A. B. ✦ Now, see, that's . . . the one thing about hearing is—

shall I tell you? I don't even remember now what I've said as the captain.

Dr. Perls ✦ So you need the tape recorder.

A. B. ✦ That's right. I don't take in. I don't take in.

Dr. Perls ✦ No, you do not absorb.

A. B. ✦ But, angel, I didn't really . . . you know I've got to say this to you . . . I really didn't come for this interview to do this.

Dr. Perls ✦ Aaaaah. . . .

A. B. ✦ Did you know? I mean that's not what I came for.

Dr. Perls ✦ That's just excuses.

A. B. ✦ That's just excuses?

Dr. Perls ✦ I've been a hundred times through this.

A. B. ✦ That's not what I . . . no. Could we go on? Please? Pretty please? Oh, women are allowed to get what they want, aren't they? No? Please? I want to. If not, the interview I had planned, I'll have to make it up.

Dr. Perls ✦ No.

A. B. ✦ I'll put in what you said at the lecture about "wiping your own ass is a sign of maturity." I got a whole dimension. But the thing is without all the living that I'd done up to now, I wouldn't have it. You know what I mean?

Dr. Perls ✦ I do know what you mean. The Gestalt Prayer says it, too.

"I do my thing, and you do your thing.
I am not in this world to live up to
your expectations.
And you are not in this world to live
up to mine.
You are you and I am I,
And if by chance we find each other,
it's beautiful.
If not, it can't be helped."

5

Behavioral Therapy

Joseph Wolpe, M.D.

Joseph Wolpe, M.D.

conceived behavioral therapy and is known throughout the world for this contribution to psychology.

He had a pious Jewish upbringing in the Union of South Africa, where his parents had immigrated as children at the beginning of the twentieth century. His M.D. thesis already showed his basic interests: it was concerned with the relationship between the conditioned responses and neurosis.

Dr. Wolpe is primarily concerned with what he calls neurotic behavior. This means any persistent learned habits in a "physiologically normal" person that prove unadaptive. This would include general feelings of anxiety, phobias, depression, and hysteria. Since Wolpe assumes that everything you are is what you have learned, he further assumes that you can unlearn it as well.

His goal of therapy is to get rid of those troublesome behaviors which are disrupting one's life, and specifically to change one's response to certain events in everyday life which cause frequent or intense anxiety. He places no limitations on his therapy in terms of age, sex, or other classifications.

Dr. Wolpe is a professor at Temple University, and head of Behavioral Science at the Eastern Pennsylvania Psychiatric Institute in Philadelphia.

Adelaide Bry ✦ You have your own theory and treatment for neuroses; based on a statement in your book, you say "neurosis obeys the laws of habit." What exactly does that mean?

Dr. Wolpe ✦ It means that neurotic behavior is learned behavior. Neuroses are essentially emotional habits that we acquire as the result of strongly anxiety-arousing experiences under certain conditions.

A. B. ✦ Do you believe it's possible to cure any neurosis by unlearning the habit that you have acquired?

Dr. Wolpe ✦ Yes, at least in principle. We don't always have available methods.

A. B. ✦ In other words, it works in part. You say that three separate processes bring change: growth, lesions, and learning. First of all, what is growth?

Dr. Wolpe ✦ What I'm doing here is distinguishing learning from other processes that change human beings. As time goes on the baby gets bigger and bigger and all sorts of things develop; such change is due to growth. "Lesions" is just another word, really, for physical disease, and you can bring about change, of course, by physical disease that in some instances brings about changed behavior. What is included here, besides actual damage to the nervous system, which would quite obviously change behavior, is change in hormones and chemical factors in the bloodstream. The form of a particular neurosis will be to some extent determined by the physical character of the individual, but the acquisition of the neurosis itself is entirely a function of learning. What you most often have is the learning of *inappropriate* or *unadaptive* *anxiety*.

A. B. ✦ This produces problems in human beings?

Dr. Wolpe ✦ It's not just that it produces problems—this anxiety most frequently *is* the problem. If, for example, you are anxious when you go into a social situation like a room full of people, then the problem that you have is anxiety—you shouldn't have anxiety in that situation. It does no good. It interferes with your function in that situation. It might also produce secondary effects in some individuals, like stuttering. Such secondary effects I suppose you could call secondary problems.

A. B. ✦ What is your theory based on then?

Dr. Wolpe ✦ The theory is that neurosis is a matter of learning. The theory of therapy is that you produce change by unlearning what has been learned in the past. One method is to help the patient to learn new habits—which may be emotional habits or thinking habits or action habits, depending on what is required.

A. B. ✦ So you take a patient and help him unlearn old habits and then help him build up a new learning process, new habits?

Dr. Wolpe ✦ I wasn't quite saying that. Let's stick to our person who has a fear of going into social situations. What he needs to do is to unlearn that fear and that's *all*. Once he ceases to fear this kind of social situation, the impairment in other behavior, speech and so on, will spontaneously be overcome. What I was saying was that, in some cases, in addition there may be a need to bring about retraining of ways of doing things, but most often it is purely a matter of overcoming the fear (i.e., anxiety) habit.

A. B. ✦ The title of your book which I have here is *Psychotherapy by Reciprocal Inhibitions*—could you define that for me? What is "reciprocal inhibitions"?

Dr. Wolpe ✦ If a person or animal has a response to a stimulus and in the presence of that stimulus you bring forward another stimulus that produces another response that is incompatible with the first response, then if the second response is stronger, it will prevent the first one from occurring. In other words, it will inhibit it. On the other hand, if the first response is stronger, then it will prevent the second one from occurring.

A. B. ◆ You take this theory that you developed and have done experimentation on animals, and you've adapted it directly to human behavior and problems—is that correct?

Dr. Wolpe ◆ Yes, most specifically with anxiety. You see, there are other responses that are incompatible with anxiety. In an animal we found that feeding was incompatible with anxiety; that if anxiety was really strong, it would inhibit or prevent feeding. If anxiety was weak and there was food present, then feeding would occur and it would inhibit the anxiety.

A.B. ◆ Don't some people eat more when they get anxiety?

Dr. Wolpe ◆ That's a *different* kind of thing. I'll tell you about that shortly. In the animal experiment, if there was just a little anxiety present and the animal was given the opportunity to eat and did eat, then the anxiety was inhibited. When this was done a number of times, it became evident that the anxiety habit was being broken down, so that finally the animal was no longer anxious even if he wasn't eating. Apparently only in children eating has a kind of emotional accompaniment which inhibits anxiey. As you say, in adults you may find that eating is being used to alleviate anxiety.

A. B. ◆ Therefore the animal experiment is not always relevant to the human.

Dr. Wolpe ◆ Well, there is always a special kind of learning history. An actual example I can give you was a ten-year-old girl who had a very strict mother by whom she was constantly being upset, particularly at mealtime. Her father used to comfort her by putting attractive morsels of food on her plate when her mother wasn't looking. This girl developed a terrific eating obsession, which means that whenever she was anxious she would turn to food—

A. B. ✦ Thinking there was the original attractive morsel of comfort on the plate.

Dr. Wolpe ✦ No, there was no need to think it. It had simply become an automatic habit.

A. B. ✦ But would it have come originally from that?

Dr. Wolpe ✦ Yes.

A. B. ✦ What would happen if I came as a patient to your office. I come to see you and I have a phobia. My phobia is fear of flying. Can we discuss treatment in terms of this phobia?

Dr. Wolpe ✦ If a person came to me with a fear of flying, I would first of all go very carefully into his whole background.

A. B. ✦ How do you go into the background?

Dr. Wolpe ✦ Some of this is very conventional. It is early home life, relationships with parents, certain neighborhood relations—all sorts of things of general background.

A. B. ✦ This is done as an interview?

Dr. Wolpe ✦ Yes.

A. B. ✦ How many interviews does it usually take to go through this conventional part?

Dr. Wolpe ✦ It is part of information-gathering, and goes with other things like going into the origin of the patient's symptoms—each one of them from the beginning. It may very well also be that a person who has a fear of flying doesn't only have that fear. Other things may be wrong, too—may or may not be. But each thing has got to be gone into in detail. We also give the patient certain questionnaires which reveal areas of disturbance that he may not even have mentioned, which may raise questions that may not have been brought up at all during the interviews. All this takes something like three or four sessions as a rule.

A. B. ✦ Then you analyze all this material and you plan a specific course of treatment?

Dr. Wolpe ✦ Yes. Treatment strategy is devised and treatment begins. If it succeeds and goes according to plan, it is pursued; and if it doesn't or if there are difficulties, the program is

reviewed and other tactics are substituted for those
originally used.

A. B. ◆ What would happen to a patient, for example, if you
discovered that this fear of flying has some problem in depth
that may be related to other things: then how is the patient
treated? Does the patient lie down or stand up? Do you give
the patient certain things to do at home? What happens now?

Dr. Wolpe ◆ What do you mean by "related to some problem in
depth"?

A. B. ◆ You said before that the fear of flying might be just a
symptom or related to other fears or other anxieties.

Dr. Wolpe ◆ No, I didn't quite say that. Indeed, it may be, but
it may not be. What I actually said was that it might not be
the *only* thing that's wrong with the patient, but that other
things may or may not have a relationship to the fear of flying.
The fear of flying may be quite isolated.

A. B. ◆ If you've gone through the four interviews with a patient
and have decided on a strategy of treatment—then what
happens to that patient when he comes for treatment?

Dr. Wolpe ◆ In the case of the fear of flying, let us assume—and
it is very important to say this—that we have determined that
it is nothing but a fear of flying. The next thing would be to
try and see what factors determine how great the fear is. It
may turn out that the patient has also got a fear of heights,
which is sort of related to the fear of flying.

A. B. ◆ Agreed.

Dr. Wolpe ◆ It may be that the patient is so afraid of planes
that even the sight of a plane on an airfield gives him anxiety,
or the sound of a plane overhead—and so you see we will then
have what is called a hierarchy of situations which produce
greater and greater fear. The most fearful situation, of course,
would be being in a plane.

A. B. ◆ Being at fifty thousand feet.

Dr. Wolpe ◆ Or maybe taking off.

A. B. ◆ How did you discover this? Was this discovered in the course of an interview?

Dr. Wolpe ✦ This is a kind of special exploration. Flying is explored to see what things externally related to flying determine the amount of anxiety; this is done in interview fashion.

A. B. ✦ What hierarchy of fears might there be in such an instance?

Dr. Wolpe ✦ Let me take an actual case in which there was a fear of heights as well as a fear of flying. What we did first was to treat the fear of heights. The patient, who incidentally had about ten other areas of disturbance, was first trained in muscle relaxation. You know how people say, "I am going to relax," and they lie down on the bed. This means they are trying to untense their muscles. Well, there is a way of doing this which goes much further than ordinary relaxing. A person can be shown how to untense muscles properly by a procedure which was introduced by Dr. Edmund Jacobson. The patient has got to be shown how to relax beyond the normal point of letting go. You know, if you try to get a muscle, like your arm muscle, to let go, you ordinarily feel, "Well, that's that—it let go." But with relaxation training, the patient is taught to take this further and further, the aim being to reach the stage at which none of the muscle fibers remains in a state of contraction.

A. B. ✦ Is he instructed to practice this muscle-relaxation therapy at home?

Dr. Wolpe ✦ He has to practice it.

A. B. ✦ So many times a day?

Dr. Wolpe ✦ He is asked to practice, usually for ten or fifteen minutes twice a day, and then when he has had sufficient training and is sufficiently skilled in muscle relaxation, it is used in what is called a desensitization process.

A. B. ✦ In the meantime, how many times is he coming for therapy while he is going through this muscle relaxation process?

Dr. Wolpe ✦ The muscle-relaxation training is done during the same interviews at which we are taking the information about the factors of the flying situation. It varies, but usually we need about three or four training sessions. In some patients one or two are sufficient; others may need six, eight, or more. But usually it's three or four.

A. B. ✦ Is he doing this in some kind of a gymnasium or just in an ordinary consultation-office?

Dr. Wolpe ✦ It is done in the chair in which you are now sitting.

A. B. ✦ I see. How would you describe this chair?

Dr. Wolpe ✦ It's a relaxing chair. It has a name: Barcalounger.

A. B. ✦ I'm going through the muscle-relaxation training at the same time you are getting the information, and now I'm ready to go into the desensitization process.

Dr. Wolpe ✦ O.K. We'll take this patient that I mentioned before.

A. B. ✦ Fine.

Dr. Wolpe ✦ First, there was the fear of height. She became anxious initially, even if she was looking out of a window on the third floor, and so in the desensitization process she was made to relax and close her eyes, and asked to imagine that she was looking out of a window on the third floor. Now, when this was imagined it produced a small amount of anxiety which she indicated. I then let her relax again and after a little while, about ten or fifteen seconds, asked her to imagine the same scene again. She did. This time the anxiety was less, and by the fourth presentation of this scene she said she had no anxiety at all.

A. B. ✦ This is in just a few minutes?

Dr. Wolpe ✦ Yes. I then asked her to imagine that she was looking out a window on the third floor, and we went through the same sequence of imagining and reporting how much anxiety there was and so forth. Soon she had no anxiety there. So then we moved up to the fourth floor, the sixth, the eighth, tenth, thirteenth, sixteenth, twentieth, thirtieth, and eventually she was able to imagine herself looking out the window of the two-hundredth floor without anxiety. The two-hundredth floor is the equivalent of about three thousand feet, which is quite high. At various parts in the course of this treatment we had checks on what she could actually do. There was a very close correlation between what she could imagine without anxiety and what she could do.

A. B. ♦ How could you check as to what she could really do?

Dr. Wolpe ♦ It was simply a matter of asking her to expose herself to various heights. For example, there was one accidental example when we had done the ninth floor. The week end after that she went to a Washington hotel and by sheer chance was offered a room on the ninth floor. She accepted that and she was perfectly comfortable. That was one kind of check.

After the heights we began to turn our attention to the specific airplane fears. She was so sensitive to planes that when she was asked to imagine a stationary plane on the airfield—this produced so much anxiety that the relaxation couldn't counter it. We had to start with her looking into a shop window and seeing a wooden plane with a six-inch wingspan. Even that produced some anxiety, but only a little.

A. B. ♦ When she sensed some anxiety, she would tell you, "I am anxious at this moment, Doctor"?

Dr. Wolpe ♦ Yes. The anxiety being produced by the wooden plane was very little. I asked her to imagine it again and it became less and less and then it became zero. So then we gradually increased the size of this plane and eventually had her imagining a large toy plane that a child could get into. And then a discarded old single-engine, single-passenger, plane, followed by larger and larger ones. Eventually she was imagining an airliner at an exhibition and then she was going into it at the exhibition, and then hearing the engine switched on merely for the sake of demonstration.

A. B. ♦ How many times did she come for therapy treatment to reach this point in her treatment?

Dr. Wolpe ✦ Actually—I must say we were treating other things at the same time at some of the same sessions. But I suppose this particular subject matter must have entered into about fifteen sessions. And, she went on to imagining that she was going for just a short hop in a plane, going no more than a couple of hundred yards. Of course, it's not an actually possible thing, but with imagination you can do these things.

A. B. ✦ Visual images can transcend reality.

Dr. Wolpe ✦ Yes. And then we had her going on real flights of twenty miles, one hundred miles, and greater and greater distances. She came to be able to imagine these things without anxiety and was in consequence enabled to go on flights without anxiety. When this woman eventually completed treatment she said that there was no place on earth where she was more relaxed than when flying.

A. B. ✦ Now, how many years has it been since she completed treatment?

Dr. Wolpe ✦ The last time I saw this woman was in 1965, and it was then three years.

A. B. ✦ After taking these imaginary flights she went on her first real flight, and then did she come back and report to you her feelings?

Dr. Wolpe ✦ Yes.

A. B. ✦ And she was perfectly fine and relaxed on the flight?

Dr. Wolpe ✦ Yes, she was.

A. B. ✦ You seem to relate a great deal of therapy to phobias. Do you feel that you are especially successful in treating this kind of patient and this kind of problem?

Dr. Wolpe ✦ There is an artificial emphasis here as a result of the approach. You see, there are lots of patients who don't come with phobias such as stuttering or fears—some have personality or character disorders. Now in the great majority of these cases, you explore and find there is anxiety which can be related to specific stimuli, so that when you do a behavior analysis the case begins to have a phobia-like form, no matter what it was like in the first place. Actually, this patient with the airplane phobia had had years and years of psychoanalysis before, and she had been regarded as a particularly complicated character-neurosis. The psycho-analyst hadn't made this kind of approach, you see.

A. B. ✦ In other words, you are saying that in order to reach the whole person, you reach that person through the specifics of a phobia.

Dr. Wolpe ✦ I am not talking about the whole person. I don't think that phrase means much. What I am saying is this: if there is a person who suffers from a neurotic reaction, specific fears form most of the basis of it, and if the fears or anxiety habits are overcome, the other problems will also disappear. If a patient stutters in social situations because of the anxiety in these situations, then if the anxiety is deconditioned, he will also not stutter in social situations.

A. B. ✦ Suppose we take stuttering as another concrete example. Doctor, how would you handle a person who stutters in social situations?

Dr. Wolpe ✦ I would discover what features of the social situations determined the amount of anxiety that control the situation, and then I would have him imagine that he is in a social situation which produces the *least* anxiety, which might be perhaps being in the presence of one strange person, and then introduce more and more strange persons.

A. B. ✦ This would be the desensitization process for stuttering?

Dr. Wolpe ✦ It might be in a particular case. In a particular kind of patient whose stutter was controlled by that kind of situation—by the presence of strangers.

A. B. ✦ I know that stuttering is considered by some therapists to be a very complex problem.

Dr. Wolpe ✦ I had one patient who stuttered to the degree that he felt in social situations that he might make a fool of himself, and so working with him I attained a list of the whole range of situations which contained this trait in different degrees.

A. B. ✦ Like what?

Dr. Wolpe ✦ One situation was where he was in a supermarket and carelessly upset a pile of cans. Another situation was in a shop where he bought some things and worked out in advance how much the purchase came to. Then the assistant worked it out and the customer—the patient—was wrong. Even though he had worked out a price higher than the real price, it was embarrassing and disturbing to him.

A. B. ✦ Whereupon he began to stutter.

Dr. Wolpe ✦ He would have stuttered to some extent. He was always particularly uncomfortable in the presence of his father. I had him imagine himself doing various things which were awkward, with his father, which included sitting in a restaurant with his father and knocking over the saltcellar. Or another situation, knocking the saltcellar down to the ground, you see, then his father displayed the attitude of contempt—anger and things like that.

A. B. ✦ So you asked the patient to go out and practice in real life.

Dr. Wolpe ✦ No, I didn't.

A. B. ✦ Oh—it was just imagining?

Dr. Wolpe ✦ Yes. The point is, it was through imagining these things while relaxed that he gradually overcame the anxiety, which means that the situations that used to make him anxious and in consequence produced his stutter, lost their power to do so.

A. B. ✦ Maybe this gets back to something we touched on a little bit before—suppose I come to you and I have another problem. I am let down and depressed, and then from that you discover that I have perhaps five or six or ten things that need to be dealt with. Are you dealing with these all at the same time? Or do you take each one separately?

Dr. Wolpe ✦ I have as my target the treatment of *all* disturbances. I might deal with several simultaneously. I would have to make a decision regarding which had priority, but it is usually several areas that would be treated simultaneously.

A. B. ✦ Since Freudian thinking is the core of most therapies, although used differently by various therapists, how would you say behavior therapy is different?

Dr. Wolpe ✦ It differs in being directed immediately towards overcoming habits, where psychoanalysts feel that these habits of fear, stuttering and so on, are due to repressed emotional complexes and that they will disappear if they derepress the complexes. So the theory of therapy and the procedures are both quite different.

A. B. ✦ Do you treat psychotics, Dr. Wolpe?

Dr. Wolpe ✦ No, I do not.

A. B. ✦ Does a patient have to be referred by a doctor, or can he just call a behavior therapist on his own?

Dr. Wolpe ✦ He can call on his own. We will then decide whether he's a suitable case or not. If he is, we try to arrange treatment.

A. B. ✦ How much does such treatment usually cost?

Dr. Wolpe ✦ It's usually based upon the therapist's fee, in much the same way as in other kinds of practice. It is so much per session. It doesn't differ at all from psychoanalysis in that respect. Of course, there are fewer sessions. Usually, the average is something like twenty or thirty sessions per patient.

A. B. ✦ That seems much less than the cost of many therapies.

Dr. Wolpe ✦ Yes. At a fee of $25, it would cost $750.

A. B. ✦ Is the family involved in behavioral therapy at all, or is it just patient and therapist?

Dr. Wolpe ✦ Well, do you mean are they directly involved?

A. B. ✦ Are they?

Dr. Wolpe ✦ As a general rule, not. But there are exceptions. There are cases in which it is necessary to bring the other person into the therapeutic situation. This applies particularly to marital problems. If, for example, the wife is distressed by a certain behavior of her husband, one of the important things to try to do would be to save the marriage, and the husband might be interviewed to enable him to understand the importance of his behavior and, if he is sufficiently motivated, try to change it.

A. B. ◆ What would you say is the future of behavior therapy in this country and throughout the world? Are you trying here in Philadelphia through Temple University or through the Institute to train more behavior therapists?

Dr. Wolpe ◆ We certainly are. It's been a very difficult matter because it's been difficult to get financial support, particularly for stipends for the trainees. There is a very rapidly rising interest and acceptance of behavior therapy. I'm sure the next few years will bring increasing support for training. I also feel, since you raise the question about the future, I feel that behavior therapy will become the normal or standard treatment for neuroses because it seems perfectly logical that if neuroses are habits, they should be tackled on the basis of the learning process and that use should be made of established knowledge of the learning process.

A. B. ◆ Have you revised your theory since you published your book in 1958?

Dr. Wolpe ◆ The basic propositions haven't changed because I think they were pretty well established by experimental work. There has been subsequent experimental work that has corroborated quite a few of the earlier findings. There have been extensions in the sense of the development of new methods from the basic theory. Also, other conditioning principles have been used in therapy. Besides this, the standard techniques, such as desensitization, have been in certain ways modified and made more efficient. My expectation is that in ten or fifteen years from now behavior-therapy techniques will be considerably different from those that are in use today, but I expect that the same basic principles will be at work.

6

Family
Therapy

Ross Speck, M.D.

Ross Speck, M.D.

has had a full, traditional career in the field of psychiatry, although he is now only in his early forties. For ten years he was Associate Professor and Head of the Section of Social Psychiatry at Hahnemann Medical College in Philadelphia, and for several years Clinical Director of the Eastern Pennsylvania Psychiatric Institute.

For the past five years Dr. Speck has been concerned with the individual as he lives in his environment, whether it be family, commune, or neighborhood. He has become a leader in the field of family therapy, trying a variety of new approaches to reach people, and even more recently he developed a theory and technique for what he terms network therapy, a way of dealing with schizophrenics and their families.

He is presently a Fellow of the Center for the Study of Social Change, New York City, and Research Associate, at the Philadelphia Psychiatric Center, concentrating on family problems.

Adelaide Bry ✦ What is family therapy?

Dr. Speck ✦ Intervening in a family system to change the family. The *family* is the unit you're treating; you're not trying to change one person, but to change the interaction among those people who are called a family.

A. B. ✦ *Called* a family?

Dr. Speck ✦ A family is really any group of people living together, headed by a mother and father, or substitutes. The newest family on the American scene is the commune. Just more people. . . .

A. B. ✦ When a family gets in trouble, does the *whole* family actually appear on your doorstep, or is it one member who comes first and says, "Hey, do something. Help! We're killing each other."

Dr. Speck ✦ One person starts it rolling—then they all come. One technique in family therapy is using *one* member to get to the rest of them.

A. B. ✦ Sounds like a lead man.

Dr. Speck ✦ It is. After the family has met once, I pick the person I feel is the healthiest, and focus on him. That way, you change the rest, since nothing stays the same if you change any part. The problem is, when you have a sick family, you have an undifferentiated family ego-mass.

A. B. ✦ Undifferentiated family ego-mass . . . that's a big phrase.

Dr. Speck ✦ In sick families, there is only one ego; in healthy families, each person is unique, strong in his own right. Sick families are appendages of one another, all stuck together. . . .

A. B. ✦ And you unstick them . . . what do you talk about with the healthiest family member?

Dr. Speck ✦ I get him to talk about his feelings about the others, who in the family he hates, tolerates, what hurts, what is impossible. But one rule—no past history. He has to talk about *here* and *now*.

A. B. ✦ I see that person as a kind of tattletale on the family. But lucky. He can get the anger out.

Dr. Speck ✦ And . . . when he expresses that anger (and sometimes good feelings) he becomes stronger, with the therapist's support. My job is to develop a strong "I" position, a stronger sense of self. Then he goes back to the family and says "*I* feel, *I* want, *I* need, *I'm* going to get."

A. B. ✦ Automatically, that changes the positions and the players. . . .

Dr. Speck ✦ When one of the so-called appendages becomes more independent, it throws the old balance out of whack. They're amazed; they have to look at him in a new way, then at themselves, and the change begins. . . .

A. B. ✦ That's just *one* technique in family therapy.

Dr. Speck ✦ There are many. . . . One is isolating one or more areas of communications problems, like money, or neatness, or eating. I play roles, we use psychodrama, everyone watches the others doing their "uncommunicating." It's a short approach; it works. Another emphasizes nonverbal communication. You ask the family members to touch each other, change seats, move around the office, sit on the floor. Something unexpected will happen to break into the old rigid system. It's like a surprise, and it wakes them up.

A. B. ✦ What's your particular way?

Dr. Speck ✦ Flexible, I hope! I like to see the whole family; even aunts, uncles, lawyers, priests, need to be included sometimes. If part of a particular family system is absent, the rest are resistant to change. I may at times work with the marital couple alone, the children alone, or any subgroup . . . depending. I try with every family to visit that family once in their home. It started about twelve years ago when an associate of mine began to visit sick families because we couldn't get the schizophrenic member out. He was usually locked in his room, and we had to resolve the psychosis in that one family member. You wear their resistance down as a starter because they're comfortable in their own home.

A. B. ✦ What else do you get from visiting the home?

Dr. Speck ✦ Visible and invisible influences. When the barricaded person is in his room, I go up. You see pets which are an extension of the family personality and can be extremely neurotic. You see who eats together, sleeps together. And that's strange. Because Mommy and Daddy are often sleeping with various children, not with each other. In a middle-class living room there's always one overstuffed chair which *should* belong to Daddy; sometimes a small child has usurped it because in a disturbed situation, the father is not acting his role of parent. Once I found a death room; grandmother had died seven years before, the family thought the room was inhabited by ghosts, and no one slept there even though three grown sons were occupying one small room next to it. I even poke into closets.

A. B. ✦ Sounds time-consuming.

Dr. Speck ✦ It is...and because of that, after that one visit to the home to get the picture...then we meet in my office... My strategy is to set out just enough seats in advance for the number who are coming and allow them to pick their own place. This tells me a great deal about the pecking order in the family, and the relationships and the amount of chaos.

A. B. ✦ I see you have a variety of chairs, overstuffed, easy, straight-back. . . .

Dr. Speck ✦ I use these chairs and play detective. If a seven-year-old takes the biggest, most comfortable chair, and his nine-year-old sister takes the next most comfortable chair, and in a subtle sort of way directs the father to a hard straight chair, or in one case even had him sitting on the edge of the couch, this tells me right off who is doing the

parenting. Sometimes a kid will try for my chair. I say,
"I'm *Dr. Speck*, this is my office—move over!" So I see the
kids running the situation because of the disorganization
and role-abdication of the parents.

A. B. ♦ Someone had to fill the vacuum....

Dr. Speck ♦ And the chair game is surprisingly accurate in the
information it reveals. The family is probably the root of both
evil and good. It's the unit that socializes people in our
society; once you've learned Western family life, you've also
accepted the madness of most Western social institutions.
In a way, it's mad to be sitting in my paneled office. We might
be better off in the park...but it's not realistic, so here
we are....

A. B. ♦ Any unusual openings for conversation when the family
group gathers and has sat down?

Dr. Speck ♦ Recently I saw a family of two middle-aged parents
and four children. The twenty-eight-year-old daughter, living
at home, had been labeled a schizophrenic. They picked their
seats; the labeled girl went into a corner. I started the
conversation by asking "What is the trouble in this family?"
Then I slowly looked around at each person, and by varying
my gaze, I was asking no one person in particular, but the
entire family as a unit. In this family group, the labeled one
was shabbily dressed; she had a kind of state-hospital
appearance, and the first thing she did when she sat down was
lift up her dress, put it over her head, and keep it there.

A. B. ♦ How did you react?

Dr. Speck ♦ I looked at her calmly, showed no surprise, and
asked again, "What is the trouble here?" No answer. Then I
said, "How am I to help you if you won't talk?" (This was
directed towards everyone.) The family coughed and
giggled, and began pointing towards the girl with the dress
over her head. Then I said, "Well, what are you trying to
tell me?" Somebody opened up: "Well, Doc, look at her, she's
crazy." I answered, "I don't know that she's crazy; she looks

like an all-American girl to me." With that, a moment later,
I saw the edge of the dress come creeping down; an eye
appeared, and I even saw a grin on her face.

A. B. ✦ You *shocked* the family into another way of looking at
her.

Dr. Speck ✦ I did—it was a good start for this family because
the labeled one, the outsider, was already beginning to be
involved. Her thoughts, no matter how fragmented, were
already turning in the direction of "Hey, what's going on here?
Here's somebody who thinks maybe somebody in the family
is nuts *besides* me," and there's the beginning of a relationship.

A. B. ✦ You made contact by moving the labeling process, and
they saw that the doctor didn't agree with their homemade
diagnosis.

Dr. Speck ✦ And I set up an early alliance with the labeled one.
Maybe no one ever before had tried to see her as just another
person in the family. I'm saying, "I'm doing the labeling here.
Doesn't every girl pull her dress up over her head every once
in a while?"

A. B. ✦ How did the mother and father take it?

Dr. Speck ✦ Very defensively. But I immediately asked,
"What are you defending against? I want to know what *your*
hangups are. She looks so normal to me that I don't think we
have to work with her. *You're the ones.*" Then I began to
work on the processes that were happening in the rest of the
family unit. Most times, the family gets pretty uptight.
So you have to work inconsistently and consistently.

A. B. ✦ In all directions, hitting hard to break them down . . .
the spotlight has moved.

Dr. Speck ✦ They're scared; they're out from under cover
themselves. But the job isn't to kill the parents. That's too
easy. It's to examine all of the relationships within the family
unit. Here I'm using nonverbal messages. I'm not fixed in
my chair in a family therapy session. I get up, wander around,
sit in another place, so when I find role relationships are stuck,

I can move them.

A. B. ✦ Role relationships stuck?

Dr. Speck ✦ Fixed orders of behavior which are often handed down from generation to generation, and then sick families beget sick families. Fixed orders of behavior can start at any time. Margaret Mead was one of the first people to carefully arrange the seating at conferences to get the utmost of interactions and to freely change the seating when she saw two people sitting together who perhaps overpowered the group, or separated themselves. When you have a conference or seminar that runs weekly, you know that within the first ten minutes the process is set, and it's never going to change unless someone is perceptive enough to say, "If we want to have an innovative, ongoing, freewheeling conference, we are going to change seating, get different personalities at the head of the table, and get the silent one at the end somewhat more in the middle and shake it up. Several times during a family therapy session I jump up and say, "I want to sit here next to you." It could be any member of the family.

A. B. ✦ Just that changes the relationships?

Dr. Speck ✦ People communicate differently immediately; they loosen up. The basic job is to loosen up the old rigid structure. This is the systems theory. It's like billiard balls properly aligned on a table and you have to do the break. I do it several times. I used to do longer-term family therapy than I do now.

A. B. ✦ How long do you do it now?

Dr. Speck ✦ Anywhere from twelve to twenty sessions. I used to do it in a more psychoanalytic way and that took longer.

A. B. ✦ What does that mean?

Dr. Speck ✦ I worked on resistances, defenses, and transference with each member of the family. It was too long, too slow. It may be necessary in certain obsessional types of schizophrenic persons, or serious character disorders or deep neuroses. In the vast majority of families, a direct approach

like we've been talking about brings about some change in the
first ten sessions.

A. B. ◆ Once a week?

Dr. Speck ◆ Usually.

A. B. ◆ One hour . . . or longer?

Dr. Speck ◆ One hour usually. Sometimes two hours. Some
families take time to warm up. But you're not going for
insight. You're not going for understanding the structural
aspects of the mental apparatus or how the defenses operate.
You're trying to get change going in *one* family member.
Once you do, the theory, like the domino theory, is when the
change starts, the others must change. What I do is focus on
one, two, or even three areas of relationships and
communication. I'll stick to that, I won't let the family escape,
I'll make concrete suggestions about jobs, about moving out
of the home, about . . . almost anything.

A. B. ◆ You give direct advice in family therapy? That's a real
taboo in psychoanalysis.

Dr. Speck ◆ It's the opposite. When I started doing
psychotherapy, I was more passive, and it's still possible in
one-to-one therapy, but direct intervention has been a part
of family therapy since its inception nearly twenty years ago.
The degree of intervention depends of course upon the
individual therapists, and we're definitely not in competition
with readers, advisors, and numerologists!

A. B. ◆ Family therapy hours sound busy—even noisy.

Dr. Speck ◆ No question. It's a dynamic hour. After the ten or
twenty sessions, you give them a breather to see what
happens, and you may get them back in three months or six
months to reinforce what they've learned. Sometimes I'll
demonstrate. For example, take a weak and passive father who
abdicates his role in the family, where mother is mother and
father too; she loves to control and dominate and at the same
time is contemptuous of the father's weakness. I'll naturally
encourage him to stand up to her, but if it doesn't work, I'll

tell him to sit back and watch and be therapist, and I'll act the husband. I'll stand right up to her and demonstrate various ways of dealing with her, and I'll get her feelings and her feedback about how she feels when she's treated in a subordinate role. Then we'll have rehearsals and I'll ask the husband to act his part—in a new way.

A. B. ✦ In individual therapy, people go for months, sometimes even years, to change. How can this therapy work so quickly?

Dr. Speck ✦ I think it's a matter of goals. Individual psychotherapy usually aims at insight, understanding one's personal mental operations. I think individual therapy often gets fixated at adjusting patients to the existing social order, to "normality" . . . whatever that is.

A. B. ✦ What's the specific goal in your family therapy?

Dr. Speck ✦ *Change*. Modifying family tensions and troubles. Changing relationships which produce pain. Just taking a new position to the people they deal with day in and day out.

A. B. ✦ So they'll destroy each other less? A matter of small degree?

Dr. Speck ✦ Hopefully. Occasionally the goal of family therapy might be to actually break up the family. Not often, but once in a while it has to be done.

A. B. ✦ Presumably the motivation that would bring the whole family in your office would be really acute daily misery.

Dr. Speck ✦ True. Besides, a lot of these families have had individual members in individual therapy, thinking that would solve the family problem. But it didn't. That's the greatest number of case referrals. They've tried whatever they've heard about. I feel strongly that psychotherapy in this country borrowed too heavily from the psychoanalytic model. As an investigation in depth of the person, his psychology, his relationships in the world, Freud reiterated over and over that it does not promise cure, or even have cure as a primary goal.

A. B. ✦ You feel then that psychoanalysts turned research into an office practice.

Dr. Speck ✦ Just because the extent of the theory is more complete than any other theoretical model that I know, people began to take it *literally*. Psychiatrists after World War II began to conduct "psychoanalytically oriented psychotherapy" on their patients once or twice a week, and now you had a diluted five-times-a-week psychoanalysis with too many built-in pitfalls and cure-expectations.

A. B. ✦ By contrast, your family therapy seems to be based on a behavioral model. Change your behavior and you'll then change your family relationships.

Dr. Speck ✦ All therapies, whether they say so or not, are based to some extent on the behavioral model. I'm not an expert on behavioral therapy, but I see that role-conditioning, reward kinds of approaches and gratifications are all used in family therapy.

A. B. ✦ I sense you have a great feeling of freedom in trying new ideas with families. What are some of the offbeat things you've done?

Dr. Speck ✦ I think I've gotten younger as I've gotten older. Sometimes when I see a stiff and rigid family after they've seated themselves, I just lie right down on the floor and look up at the ceiling . . .

A. B. ✦ I bet that gets a strong response.

Dr. Speck ✦ It shakes them up. I'll even encourage some of them to get down on the floor; of course with rigid families, it's difficult. Sometimes I'll leave the room, get them to talk together. I'll go for a walk. When I have facilities, I'll watch through a one-way mirror and, with a microphone, speak back and forth, giving them instructions about how to relate to one another. With psychotic patients, I'll get into it . . . from the inside. Once I had a family with religious obsessions; they even wondered whether vitamins were kosher. The twenty-three year-old son was schizophrenic, and he had formed a new religion. So I became his first convert. After six weeks of pretending to take his religious instruction in the therapy sessions, the family called the director of the hospital with which I was associated, to announce that I'd gone crazy . . . But when we got it straightened out, the family was *clearly* aware of their pathology. So I'll swing out crazier than anyone, if that strategy will work; talking psychotic language is a dramatic lesson to the family.

A. B. ✦ You talk a lot about the rigid family. Is that a lot of us in America today?

Dr. Speck ✦ The American family is in trouble.

A. B. ✦ How?

Dr. Speck ✦ In an age of social change, like now, the nuclear family is kind of like God and country, and stamped with the American flag. If you say anything negative . . . you can be negative—and . . .

A. B. ✦ You mentioned the *nuclear* family . . .

Dr. Speck ✦ The nuclear family . . . parents and their children, and they live together in a box called a house and they travel together in a box called a car and are quite isolated and walled off from their fellow men and, today, they are in deep trouble. All family therapists are concerned about the survival of the institution itself, and about whether it is possible to change the family sufficiently so it will survive in the post-technological world. Now experiments are going on attempting to go back to the old communal type of family, which existed up until the Industrial Revolution. The nuclear family today is being challenged by young people under thirty . . . and even some over. The trouble is, the family is so crucial to all of western man's thought because the role-types of mother, father, sister, brother, are perpetuated through every institution from church to industry, to social relationships. So, even in communes, what arises is a pseudo mother, father . . . the same thing happens on a bigger scale.

A. B. ✦ Is it better, though, because more people are in it?

Dr. Speck ✦ *The tribe is better.* It's more people, less loneliness.

A. B. ✦ Is part of the family's problem too few people

living in that box?

Dr. Speck ✦ Too separated. The world is just too complicated and very few people understand enough of it to program enough of it into their children to prepare them for the future. The old communal families were seventy or one hundred persons.

A. B. ✦ Did that produce fewer neuroses than what we have today?

Dr. Speck ✦ I think significantly less.

A. B. ✦ In most nuclear families there's always one really sick person . . .

Dr. Speck ✦ That's the scapegoat . . . the one everyone pins their own problems on.

A. B. ✦ Do even so-called normal families have scapegoats?

Dr. Speck ✦ I think scapegoating is universal, dating back at least to Abraham and Isaac and probably back to Cain and Abel.

A. B. ✦ But you're still trying to help the scapegoated one get unscapegoated.

Dr. Speck ✦ Or antiscapegoated—to fight!

A. B. ✦ If every family needs a scapegoat, and you unscape that one, who gets the blame then?

Dr. Speck ✦ It can be shared, it can be a role that wanders, that doesn't reside in one person. In psychotic or schizophrenic familes, one socially useful function of the scapegoating is so that the other members in the family can function. That's a pretty big price for one person to pay. For family life to be healthier and happier, we have to get large changes in social organizations. We have to get rid of a lot of our mythologies, starting with religion and ending up with some of our conventional beliefs about family life, apple pie, etc. . . .

A. B. ✦ While we're waiting for those big changes, what's my clue as to whether I should bring my family now for therapy? What's my concrete reason?

Dr. Speck ✦ A variety of reasons. Some people's tolerance for pain in the family is greater than others. In my experience (of course, I have a reputation for working with psychotic families), it's a predicament I can only describe as everyone being wedded to everyone else in "unholy bliss."

A. B. ◆ The specific predicament?

Dr. Speck ◆ Such pain that one loves one's offspring so much that one can never be out of their presence, has never had a babysitter, cannot go downtown or to the movies because one feels so horribly guilty that Johnny is suffering at home, and is feeling so terrible that once one leaves the confines of the house for twenty feet, one becomes terror-stricken, panic-stricken, full of guilt, and then runs home to fight with the other members.

A. B. ◆ They are so *close* physically and emotionally. . . .

Dr. Speck ◆ That they don't have a chance to grow individually. No one can breathe or form relationships outside. Sometimes the father goes around the house constantly from room to room, seeing what everyone is doing, even knocking on bathroom doors, so there's no privacy; it's *intense* emotional involvement. It's like a small mental hospital, and the problem is there's no *person* in the family. You have to make persons.

A. B. ◆ Is that what a really sick family is?

Dr. Speck ◆ Yes, and in that environment where one person has been diagnosed as psychotic, he's living in his own world in preference to dealing with the family, but of course, they're sick too.

A. B. ◆ A family should come early in the game. . . .

Dr. Speck ◆ As early as possible. Some of these problems show up by the time the children are nine. They're not involved, there's a lack of joy in themselves and others. The kids are already beginning to live out the frustrated myths of the parents. Often, the child is making his last feeble attempts at autonomy, and this is seen as a form of sickness: "He's trying to break away from us."

A. B. ✦ What are these myths?

Dr. Speck ✦ The child becomes not only what he is told verbally, but nonverbally, he lives out the ghosts of his parents. The problem is that parents and then grandparents have done this to parents. People have investigated three to five generations of sick families and see the dreadful thing happen over and over. The basic role of the family is to *undo* itself, to let the members out, to be individuals. At the same time, by its very nature, even at its healthiest, the love and hate bonds and binds, and pulls people into a kind of guilty hate-filled love.

A. B. ✦ If you were running a healthy family, letting them undo their bonds, how would you do it?

Dr. Speck ✦ I would give them much greater freedom than we've ever considered before. As a parent of seven children, and having grown up in this culture, I certainly fall into many of the pitfalls that other people do. It's almost impossible to escape them all. But I *try* to listen to my children, to learn from them, instead of being so anxious to program *into* them what I learned from my parents. The best alternative is the commune family, and they're coming for family therapy these days.

A. B. ✦ *Whole communes come for therapy? Why?*

Dr. Speck ✦ The commune is new and anything new is painful, a different experience than they were programmed to know. But I hope that family therapists won't put their hangups onto the communes, but will hang loose in seeing their own shortcomings and see if this is a viable model for preparing people who will be alive, experiencing minds and bodies. There will not be this schizoid split where people don't have much in their bodies anymore.

A. B. ✦ People don't have *bodies* anymore?

Dr. Speck ✦ Well, not much in the way of bodies. Feeling is very constricted. People are very uptight. You just have to look at people on the street, in crowds. The joy has gone out of people.

A. B. ✦ Since the majority of middle-class America still lives in the nuclear family, what can they do to make it more possible for these three, four, five people to live together in harmony?

Dr. Speck ◆ The secret is probably all tied up within the family, with the *images*. You see, we are all ghosts of our past. We have all taken into us the significant people, the people who have guided our lives. They are still ruling us and running us. We are trapped. What people *can* do is to *try to keep free and open communication going, to try to drop rigidities of values and modes of existence. They can try.* What Grandma did should be dropped. I think families do change. People who do come to the family therapist get a growing edge on close human relationships which they are then going to have to nurture.

A. B. ◆ What's your vision of the future of family therapy?

Dr. Speck ◆ Perhaps better than other kinds. It's not rigidified, it's not ossified in dogma. The research is leading in the directions of understanding social networks of all kinds, of quick crisis intervention. We're all caught in this rapid social change, and in order to survive, we have to adapt. For joy in human life . . . in the family, which has at the moment atrophied in the name of progress, we, as family therapists, can help this human family feel freer. Family therapy has gone through a lot in its twenty years, and it will no doubt undergo as much upheaval as the family of mankind does in the next twenty years.

7

Group
Therapy

Ian Alger, M.D.

Ian Alger, M.D.

whose current involvements vary from Consultant to St. Paul's Church, Englewood, New Jersey, to Training and Supervising Analyst, Psychoanalytic Faculty, New York Medical College, displays just that kind of range on first meeting. A trained psychoanalyst, he now devotes most of his energies to group psychotherapy because he feels that in this area more rapid changes are often possible for the human being beset by problems.

He is a dynamic, interested man, always searching for more effective methods to make people more aware and more able to deal with life.

He has all the "professional credits" one might expect. As a fellow of many top professional organizations, including the American Psychiatric Association, the American Group Psychotherapy Association, and the American Academy of Psychoanalysis, he might have remained a "conservative" in the field of psychiatry—but Alger preferred to expand his vision. He has written widely about group psychotherapy, and the use of various techniques, including videotape, which are discussed in this interview.

Adelaide Bry ✦ Dr. Alger, what kind of a psychotherapist
are you?

Dr. Alger ✦ A psychoanalyst, but one very interested in group
psychotherapy. I was trained as a psychoanalyst, but not in a
traditional way. That only tells part of it. I even use
videotape! I chose a therapist for myself who had a cultural
approach.

A. B. ✦ A cultural approach? You feel the environment has a lot
to do with what happens to a person?

Dr. Alger ✦ A person's *living* experience determines the course
of his life much more than his biology and his genetics; that's
the basis of Freudian theory: that your genetics is
all-important, although it often isn't dealt with that way.
In neo-Freudian theory your *life* experience is more important.
I moved on to develop a tremendous interest in the influence
people have one on the other and the influence cultural
traditions have on people.

A. B. ✦ One organism comes into the world and all these
influences impinge on it. . . .

Dr. Alger ✦ Enhancing or limiting the possibilities of
development, fulfillment, and growth. There's lots of evidence
for this. Maybe none of us reaches his potential; the influence
our early experience has is profound, even in stimulating our
ability to perceive. Infants exposed to color, forms, and all
kinds of activity really do seem to function at a higher
intellectual level as they grow.

A. B. ✦ Is there no way for making up for that basic lack
later on?

Dr. Alger ✦ None, so it would seem, but growth is always

possible. There is a way to achieve greater possibilities, or there wouldn't be therapists. I learned early in life that change is *always* possible; you don't need to stay in the ruts that you get into.

A. B. ◆ And you feel group therapy does the job better?

Dr. Alger ◆ I became interested in group for one reason: it seems unlikely that one person through his own effort climbs out of his rut, *especially* if everyone around wants to keep him in it. One-to-one therapy appeals to the individual's capacity, to his willpower, to his earnest interest, or to his fond hope that he's going to be able to crawl out of his rut and lead a new life in a different direction. I think it is not possible unless the *people* in his environment welcome change.

A. B. ◆ So you found that one patient sitting with you in your office didn't change enough?

Dr. Alger ◆ I still see a few people in that two-person setting, but most of my work now is devoted to groups: natural groups like family groups or business associates who group together or classes of people.

A. B. ◆ Do some groups of people who are not bound in any way just come to see you and you put them together in a group?

Dr. Alger ◆ I have groups where people come and they are strangers. I have groups of married people. Some of them are coupled together and sometimes the husband and wife go into different groups. Everyone in the group has had experience in marriage, for example, so they have that in common.

A. B. ◆ In other words, you prefer it if there is a common bond?

Dr. Alger ◆ I wouldn't say I prefer it. It's just that certain groups are structured that way. Eventually, you come down to basic issues.

A. B. ◆ How does it work, if I called you up and wanted to come to one of your groups for the first time? What happens?

Dr. Alger ◆ First, we talk together, just the two of us. Then I'd try and understand what you were looking for and what kind of experience you wanted to have and what your goals were—

how you saw your difficulties. You'd have some kind of
struggle or suffering, disappointment or desire; you want your
life to *feel* different. You may want to live differently. In the
interview that I'd have with you, I'd try to understand where
you hoped to go. At the same time I'd try to understand what
your life had been, how you'd experienced it so far, what
you'd been able to accomplish, what schooling you'd had,
what success or failure you'd had, what kind of relationships
you'd had, whether you were alone in the world right now,
or whether you felt connected with somebody; then I make an
assessment as to whether or not coming into a group would
provide a possibility for you in terms of you. If I thought so,
I'd say, "Look, I think it would help if you met in this group."

A. B. ◆ You mean you'd pick out a group that you thought I
would fit into?

Dr. Alger ◆ Right. For example, we know that in a group if
someone is depressed this is not easy for everyone around.
People around a depressed person are dragged down. If you
had a group with ten depressed people in it, you might be up
against a pretty difficult situation. No one would be able to
be a mover. To have a group function, you need people
playing different kinds of roles, fulfilling different needs of
the group. It is like a party. If you have a dull bunch of
people who are in themselves, who aren't going to respond,
it's going to be a dull evening.

A. B. ◆ At a party you need listeners and talkers.

Dr. Alger ◆ Listeners and talkers and somebody who'll get out
of a chair and move around the room or say, "Hey, let's
dance." He's a live wire so let's ask him to our party because
he will add excitement or stimulate us. Then there are people
who act as sort of sea anchors, always dragging a bit, toning
things down, and that's good too perhaps. Otherwise you may
get carried away in your enthusiasm and so you'll say "Oh,
let's not chop up the dining-room table and burn it in the
fireplace because it would be fun, but we better not."

A. B. ✦ Tell me about a group that you're involved in.

Dr. Alger ✦ Sure. I'll start with a group I have with a co-therapist. In several of my groups I work with another therapist.

A. B. ✦ A man or woman?

Dr. Alger ✦ A woman. She and I feel that we are able to accomplish more together. We feel better in the groups having shared leadership. One reason is that sometimes I want to be a participant and I don't want to be locked in the role of a leader. I feel freer if there is someone else who will move into leadership if I want to just go with what I am feeling, show my reactions, and be there as a person. It's a good feeling besides to know that someone is observing and coming in with another idea of what's going on. It is good to have two people who are able to see the same material from different points of view, even as man and woman. We often tend to see things differently. The groups like this.

A. B. ✦ If I came to one of your groups for the first time, it would probably be an ongoing group and I'd come in as a stranger not knowing anybody. What would happen to me? I might be scared.

Dr. Alger ✦ I'd ask if you had met everyone, if they knew your name, and then I'd say that the name isn't so important, it's just how we are together, but since we have names it's nice to know them. We would hope that you could be whatever you feel. There are very few ground rules. We do have a rule that we do not allow physical violence.

A. B. ✦ Do you allow touching?

Dr. Alger ✦ Certainly we allow touching. You know, being, moving, walking, sitting, standing, lying down, touching each other—no limits this way. We just don't want anyone to be hurt. We do have one assumption—that is, all of us are here with some good will towards each other: the good will of hoping the other people will grow, that we will grow, and that they will wish us well even if at times they may get angry at us. We hope that you will be able to be as open as possible about what you feel here, what you experience here, and that you share this as directly as you can.

A. B. ◆ Suppose I am afraid of telling a very personal experience, and I think even in a big city like New York this could get back to somebody. How does that work?

Dr. Alger ◆ That is a risk. There is no way to insure your confidentiality. We ask you to hold confidences that you may have about factual things that might harm us, but *there is no way to guarantee it*. To function in a group you have to risk exposure. Don't tell if you want to be 100 percent sure.

A. B. ◆ That kind of restricts the feeling, doesn't it?

Dr. Alger ◆ I don't think so, because everyone would know it's a lie if you said otherwise. I think it opens the feeling up. We take responsibility for what we are doing. This is a key thing I do, help people see that in their own awareness they have some responsibility of what happens to them. They certainly aren't able to control the direction of their lives in many ways, but to the extent that it is possible, *the more you are aware of your reactions and feelings and the more you are aware of what's going on around you and what other people are doing, what the structure of your society and the institutions in it is, the more you can be responsible in the decisions you make. The more freedom you have.*

A. B. ◆ How do I get that all important awareness? Just by being in the group and trying to listen differently?

Dr. Alger ◆ One of the ways is to communicate with other people what experiences you are having right there in the room. Of course, there is a great deal of talk of the here and now in the existential approach to therapy as well as to life. In terms of the here and now I tell my patients that the here and now is not a geographic entity. It's true that you and I are in this room and what goes on between us is here and now, but in the here and now of this moment you have a home in Philadelphia, right here, right now, and I have a family, I'm a father, I'm a husband, I'm a therapist, I'm a teacher, and all *that* is going on right now at this second and is all part of the fabric of my life. I think people very often think of the here and now as just limited to the immediate situation that they are in, but that's not true.

A. B. ✦ Everything you've been and are at the moment.

Dr. Alger ✦ There are people who may be thinking of me as their therapist right at this moment. I have a connection with them. I have a meaning and I am in that fabric. I know that this evening I am going to a business meeting of a society and at this moment I have that in my mind and how I function moment to moment now is including that information that I have to plan during the day and if something comes up all *that* is available to me. This kind of awareness of your place, of the room you're in, and the relationship you are in, relationships to friends, relationships to community, to your business, the kind of work you do, your relationship to the country, the social structure, to the world, to life.

A. B. ✦ Know what? It seems so much to deal with that maybe that's why people cop out.

Dr. Alger ✦ Obviously, you can't have it all in your immediate consciousness. People often don't have the data available to them and this is the point. It isn't available even if they want it. It doesn't come into their calculations. I'm not thinking of all this at every moment and neither are you. To the degree that I am aware of having that information available then I'll be able to retrieve it or include it in my calculations. This is what happens in a small way in the group. Suppose every time someone brings up a certain issue, you say "I know just what you mean." It sounds as if you may be empathetic with that person. And then you say, "I've had the same experience with that myself." And then you tell something of your experience. Up to this point people feel interested in what you are saying and the person you have spoken to may feel supported. Then if you go on and keep it focused on you and show no interest in the person who was talking, you are unaware of what they are feeling.

A. B. ✦ That reveals my egocentricity.

Dr. Alger ✦ You see what it reveals about you but you can see right there, perhaps, the hurt in the person who was talking. You see the discomfort in the other members of the group or the lack of it. Depending on how people experience this little drama that's going on, you can bring some more awareness to a lot of people that they are blocking out. One great difficulty most therapists have found in one-to-one therapy is that even if a person *acts differently with the therapist it doesn't mean there's going to be a carry-over*. The group is a more natural model like real life.

A. B. ✦ How long would it take me if I came to your group to get some kind of awareness? A year, three years?

Dr. Alger ✦ People come anywhere from a few sessions and leave and may get something, or may stay two or three years.

A. B. ✦ Can I come and go any time I want to?

Dr. Alger ✦ There is a responsibility to your group. If you deal with the group in a way that is damaging, perhaps the group might not like it. Suppose you come late all the time. This is disruptive. The group might challenge you. Or suppose you show up only every few sessions. The group will decide, do we want you? If they do, it is not disruptive. That's it. But if the group decides, we don't want to be in a group where people come intermittently—either come or don't come—then the person would have to decide.

A. B. ✦ And the group makes that decision?

Dr. Alger ✦ And the group makes that decision. Or I might say, "I don't want to work like this," and any member of the group could go against the group decision and say, "I don't want to work like this," and they could leave the group. Any individual could leave it. In my case I could say, "I don't want to work with it."

A. B. ✦ Do any members of the group ever get sexually

involved? Or is there a rule against it?

Dr. *Alger* ◆ Life is real and people have sexual involvements. If members of the group meet each other and have some feeling for each other, that's part of life. We aren't at the point where we have sex in the group. I guess that could be set up too; there are swinging groups, aren't there? I don't know of therapy groups having sex. I haven't heard of that. Often genitals are excluded in touching.

A. B. ◆ What about in your group?

Dr. *Alger* ◆ Well, if somebody wanted to touch somebody's genitals. . . .

A. B. ◆ Does it happen sometimes?

Dr. *Alger* ◆ Rarely, because our traditional way of dealing with each other in this society carries over into the group.

A. B. ◆ What special group techniques have you developed? I see your videotape machines.

Dr. *Alger* ◆ Video has become extremely useful in therapy, both group and individual. It simply makes use of the new technology of being able to take television pictures and play them back immediately, with equipment that is readily available. What makes it possible is it isn't exorbitantly expensive. I use it in the group in one of several ways. I may at the beginning of the group take pictures of the first ten minutes and then play that back immediately to the group and ask the group members reactions to what they see: how they see themselves—how they see others. Now we are engaged in a focused activity. We are doing something. We are looking at these pictures and responding. That's much better than saying, "Well, let's just react with one another in a free-flowing way." Sharing feelings and reactions and observations about this common experience in itself is therapeutic.

A. B. ◆ Is that how it's immediately helpful?

Dr. *Alger* ◆ One person may just have been talking and another person was looking away and when you play it back, a person says, "Hey, look at you on the screen, you aren't *listening* to me at all." And the person who was looking away says, "It's true, I didn't realize that it showed, but obviously I'm bored, looking away."

A. B. ✦ You can't fake or rationalize.

Dr. Alger ✦ Then someone else would say, "What *were you* thinking about?" This may lead to a further revelation about what was going on and then the rest of the group may begin to wonder about the lack of attention. Was it boring? Was the first person doing something the group wanted to avoid? Why was there difficulty? If there is any question about what happened, all we do is turn on the videotape and see it. You can play it back and focus on the person who was talking and then focus on someone else the next playback and you begin to tease out the intricate pattern of intercommunication and interbehavior going on. Everybody begins to realize that no piece of behavior is isolated. This is exciting! In the old traditional therapy if a person is silent for ten minutes, there is a tendency to understand silence in terms of the inner workings of that person's psyche. Newer communication theory says, "Look, we can't understand a person's silence by looking inside that person." You have to see what is happening outside, what other people were doing at that time. Did anyone show any interest in hearing an opinion from that person, for instance? Were there cues given that shut that person out? Maybe that person got a real cold shoulder. Or as one person is talking, each time he would say something perhaps the other person would have raised his hand giving stop signals, which pass in ordinary discourse and nobody recognizes. These are the kind of data that talk-oriented therapy is very little interested in. No behavior can be understood in isolation.

A. B. ✦ A whole new dimension.

Dr. Alger ✦ Right. This whole realm of communication and seeing is the trend of our last years of the sixties. This is where we are moving with videotape cassettes. We are going to have small video cameras and people are going to photograph their behavior. Sort of immediate retrieval. It's going to do something home movies could never do. The whole underground movement in videotape now is gaining popularity and publicity. There are videotapes taken with small portable cameras on the streets. Or they will go into places of entertainment and take rock players just doing their thing as it is happening.

A. B. ✦ Do you think with videotape that people can change more drastically because they have a new dimension with which to assess their behavior?

Dr. Alger ✦ This brings an entirely different kind of awareness. It's what McLuhan has been talking about. Information is transmitted *less* through the written word, and *more* with picture and sound as things are happening. We experience war now very differently than we ever have because of the videotape. It is revolutionary. The more we *see*, the more we understand, the more capability we have to do things differently.

A. B. ✦ Have you seen since you started to use videotape in 1965 that change and growth in people is more rapid or more definite?

Dr. Alger ✦ It's hard to pin it down. I do feel now in my practice people are making more rapid shifts and changes, but I've been doing *many* different things and can't say it is just due to video. It is all connected to ways of trying to increase a person's awareness of reality. Videotape helps. The playback at the beginning increases the kind and intensity of the involvement and the cohesiveness of the group.

A. B. ✦ I really have accepted new realities because I can't deny this that I *see!*

Dr. Alger ✦ In this way you create more of an investigative attitude towards yourself and others. This is the atmosphere I create in groups, in therapy and in life, too: a connection with people which says I am interested, I understand and see what

is happening, and I'm also interested in giving you my
reaction. If somebody is rude to me, I'm not going to respond
by saying, "Gee, that's interesting." I react immediately with
my feeling. Helping people become more aware of their
feelings and the reaction they are getting and encouraging
them to express it directly can be misapplied and is often
misunderstood in therapy. People may get the idea that they
can go into their lives and—outside group—come out directly
with whatever responses they want.

A. B. ◆ People do get that out of group sometimes.

Dr. Alger ◆ This is inappropriate and gets you into a hell of a
lot of trouble. Life is more complex than that. There is a large
difference between having an awareness available to yourself
and then deciding either in your own full consciousness, or
perhaps automatically after you get used to it, but deciding
whether you are going to use it. You may be aware of anger,
but you have a choice of how you are going to express the
anger, and if you don't take the context into account, the
world will not accept you.

A. B. ◆ Some people say they learn to be themselves in group—
then they go into the outside world and find it difficult
because they can't be real.

Dr. Alger ◆ There are very few places where all kinds of
directness and openness are welcome. I try to help people see
that once they are aware of their own reactions, they also need
skill in assessing other people. A *lot* of work in therapy
doesn't deal just with a person's inner feeling but with what is
going on in the world, what sort of games go on. What is the
real motive of people? People don't have *just* good will
towards one another. Let's see what's happening. What is the
setup? Knowing more, how can you best deal? Perhaps you
can even alter the outer setup. For example, I was chairman of
a meeting. Now, often chairmen have difficulty in cutting
speakers off and you will see them up there sweating and,
below, fidgeting, is the audience—caught. In therapy you learn

that it is possible to function in a way which need not be abusive, yet still be effective in your role as chairman. In one meeting I was able to actually interrupt in the middle of a sentence. You don't have to follow every cue that's given. We are trained and we tend to automatically follow cues.

A. B. ✦ Like conditioned animals.

Dr. Alger ✦ We really are, I think, following nonverbal cueing behavior up to 80–90 percent of the time. There are hundreds of cueing and signaling motions and pieces of behavior per second in any interchange. No one could be consciously aware of all that. The most we can do is to be able to master certain large cues. See then if we can begin to shift.

A. B. ✦ You said there were other techniques that you used in groups besides videotape. What are they?

Dr. Alger ✦ One is the use of dream interpretation, a classic technique; everyone shares their associations and their reactions. One thing about dreams; the symbols or the mythology of the dream are drawn not just from our personal experience. There is cultural mythology and symbolism, and we can understand each other's symbolic language; if someone tells you a dream, you don't need necessarily to know every association that he has to his dream in order to get some feeling about what that story may be saying. So I have people who really respond with their reactions to a dream. This can be very enlightening. We use fantasy and ask someone to give a daydream to open up their feelings. Any technique which helps a person open up to himself to understand his own feelings and gives a clearer understanding of the groups that he is in, of other people, is useful. *If anything characterizes my therapy, it's that all these techniques are used in a very personal, human context.* We try to see each other in the group as other persons and that underlies everything. Anything which dehumanizes, I try to avoid. Television could be used in a dehumanizing way. You could use it to try to force ideas on a person. You could beat them with it. You could say, *"Look* at what you are doing. Now look at that again!'' It isn't just the technique, but it's whether you can use it in a mutually respectful, cooperative human interaction.

A. B. ◆ You want to help a person grow and make shifts in his life. Do you think sometimes people in group therapy feel they must go out and *do* something very different in order to prove that they are now different?

Dr. Alger ◆ I think people could hope that my groups would not have that as one of their values. This brings up the whole question of force of a group. Of growth, but also of the force, the coercive group force. That in itself is another technique, which can be used destructively or positively. If the force of a group has respect for each individual's life, it will welcome individuation as well as compliance. But if the group becomes a coercive force to try to push a point of view—if, for instance, someone isn't *allowed* to be silent—then the group can be extremely coercive; nobody can really withstand for very long the total disapproval of the group he is in. He must either wither in some way or escape if possible.

A. B. ◆ That seems to depend on the skill of the therapist.

Dr. Alger ◆ It's very delicate. There is no mechanical way to talk about it; you have to get the feel of each individual situation and see if there is a humanity here or is there an authoritarian coerciveness which is used as a way to oppose a human approach. A human approach is one which respects another individual's way to be himself and to have his autonomy. It obviously depends on the therapist because it is related to his value-system: how he sees other people and how he feels about them.

A. B. ◆ How do you define personal growth?

Dr. Alger ◆ I see a person's developing his capacity to have respect for himself as a person, to be less blaming towards himself, to be less harsh in terms of how he will accept his own humanness and his own functioning and in terms of his attitude towards his fellows: whether he has to control them and coerce them, or whether he can see other people as being individuals who have a direction of their own with whom he may be able to have a kind of relationship.

A. B. ✦ In other words, a feeling of acceptance for oneself and others on a pretty deep level. . . .

Dr. Alger ✦ On a deep level . . . now he's able to go out and live, if he also has an awareness of the world around him. To the degree he is ignorant of the realities of life, he is going to be terribly handicapped.

A. B. ✦ What are *the* realities of life? The realities are very different for each of us.

Dr. Alger ✦ Very different, but very much the same, too, and this is what group can help with.

A. B. ✦ What do you feel are the realities of life?

Dr. Alger ✦ That work is important, that things don't just fall in our laps as we expect them to. The realities are that we live in an extremely complex society which is very difficult to move within in certain ways. That there isn't much welcoming for many aspects of humanness and that people are not personally to blame because of it. I spoke to a man in an elevator this morning who was a professional person in administration. We passed the time of day and he said, "How are you?" and I said, "Fine," and I said, "How is your life?" and he said, "OK." That's the kind of conversation you have on elevators. And then I said, "Well, you know I'm struggling to find a little bit of living here and there and it isn't too oppressive." And he said, "Well, I am too but it isn't very easy." And he said, "It seems my sense of privacy is invaded on every hand. I feel harried and have hardly any time that I feel I can even know myself or what's happening." So that is a different kind of conversation than we usually have in elevators and I felt for a moment we made contact, which felt good to me. I said, "I guess moments like this may be where we can find some meaning here and there."

A. B. ✦ That kind of openness is happening?

Dr. Alger ✦ Yes, there is an attempt to reach each other in this human, caring way. I feel this is the thrust of our whole future value-system: to value each other and to care for each other as human beings, rather than the accumulation of material possession or status, which I think has been very much the thrust. Everything is being questioned. Therapy is being questioned, institutions are being questioned.

A. B. ✦ How do you feel about the future of therapy?

Dr. Alger ✦ I still call myself a psychoanalyst, but I feel there is room for theoretical change, growth, and movement. The way therapy has been practiced, not just psychoanalysis, there has been a very *authoritarian* approach. It was based in part on the medical model where the doctor was an expert and saw it was easy for the patient to play the passive role; this was carried over into psychotherapy. When the couch was used and the patient was lower than the doctor, this symbolized that position, and to this day, there still are many things in the context of therapy which cue in this lower role. I think as a therapist I do have some understanding of certain techniques and some understanding about life which I hope can be useful to a person. So, we aren't equal exactly, maybe in our understanding of certain things. But, on the other hand, anyone I've seen may have it over me in many ways too in his understanding of the realities of the world. So, I can't even claim superiority in that sense.

A. B. ✦ You're not claiming the traditional role of put-down.

Dr. Alger ✦ The fact that I charge does create a difference. How can you be an equal or a peer and charge something? If I need to consult a lawyer, I consult him and yet I want to be dealt with as a peer. I think this whole model of therapy has shifted very much recently from father-son, father-daughter roles to more like a brother-sister or brother-brother role. The commonness of our humanity and the recognition that we are all involved in the same kind of dilemma and that we can reach out to one another in the midst of our puzzlement—this struggle is the new thrust in therapy, and in the whole human experience we are having together.

A. B. ◆ You really *live* your work!

Dr. Alger ◆ I feel hopeful in a personal way; I have found through my work a closeness to many people, and I feel my life has greater fullness and richness in it and I feel better. I feel happier in a sense; even if I am unhappy, I'm happier. If I'm angry, I'm happier. By happy I mean I feel more involved and in touch with other people. I am more aware of my humanity and I like that. I like to live that way. In a sense, I really do feel more ready to die than I ever have because I've had experience in living this way. I don't think of death with any bitterness. It doesn't feel cruel or unfair. It is like I've welcomed what I've experienced and I don't feel cheated any more.

A. B. ◆ Why do you say *any more?*

Dr. Alger ◆ I used to feel cheated. I used to feel I wouldn't want to die, that I hadn't really somehow lived in a way that made any sense. It isn't that it has to make great sense conceptually, but it makes sense in a feeling way to me. I'm glad I've had this experience. I was able to let people touch my life, I think that's more it, and then I was able to touch theirs. As a therapist I opened up my own life more to my patients and my own reactions, my own humanity, which is something I try doing . . . When you ask what other techniques I use, this is one of the crucial things I've tried to do in therapy . . . *include myself in the process.* As I've said, you can't understand any person alone, so that in a two-person therapy, you can't understand the patient without understanding what the therapist is doing at that time and how he's feeling. So, I've tried to tell my feelings to my patients, let them know what is going on with me as they are having certain feelings and experiences with me, and what is happening in my life. I try to be a person with my patients. And as I've done that, I've found that they treat me in a very different way and they warm me, and they understand and they can have compassion for me and they can get angry at me, and they can be disappointed in me and they can tell me about it and I feel much more real and much more in touch. They do too. I think this is one of the crucial ways that human development occurs. It was at first through this kind of experience that I became interested in videotape, because it allowed me through another modality to include more of myself and my behavior in the data that we are going to look at in therapy. We aren't just looking at the patient then as a subject of investigation; we are examining and trying to understand our total human involvement.

8

Encounter Group Therapy

Frederick Stoller, Ph.D.

Frederick Stoller, Ph.D.

who died suddenly of a heart attack, in June 1970, was in his early forties and a leader in the encounter group movement.

He had originally been a psychoanalytically oriented psychotherapist, working in traditional ways. As he began to experiment with the group process, he felt strongly that "group workshops represent a place where you can get refreshed and return to life."

Stoller was Associate Professor in the School of Public Administration at the University of Southern California.

His professional career, for a relatively young man, was broad in scope; he had researched and written widely.

Adelaide Bry ✦ Dr. Stoller, *father* of the encounter group.

Dr. Stoller ✦ Not really. I am one of the original pioneers of the *marathon* group, a particular kind of encounter group which runs rather continuously over a period of time, generally a weekend. Five or six years ago I was one who visualized the potency of that kind of group.

A. B. ✦ What is this potency?

Dr. Stoller ✦ Let me make a couple of distinctions here. The *encounter* group is a general name. A marathon is a particular arrangement in hours. That is when it runs continuously for an hour or two, breaks up, and then the group comes back at a later time.

A. B. ✦ For a total of . . .?

Dr. Stoller ✦ Generally, the minimum marathon runs at least eighteen hours. Others run about thirty to thirty-six hours, usually starting on Friday evening and ending somewhere Sunday afternoon. The encounter group has its origin in group psychotherapy, which has been around for fifty years. It really became important in the fifties and sixties as a form of treatment. In group psychotherapy the major emphasis is upon problems the person brings to the setting. People focus in on the problems, and they try to solve the problems and try to help the person understand why he's getting into the kind of difficulty he's getting into.

A. B. ✦ You tell yours, I tell mine. Is that it?

Dr. Stoller ✦ Yes. Group psychotherapy assumes you have a problem and asks, "What is it?" Now the encounter group, as a group, will often look exactly like a psychotherapy group— if you walked into the middle of it you might not be able to tell the difference between the two—but the basic assumption is not that you have a problem, but that you've come to learn something about yourself. The idea is the more you know yourself, the more you're able to enrich your life.

A. B. ✦ In other words, you don't have to be fearful, anxious, depressed, or *anything*.

Dr. Stoller ✦ You may actually just be saying ,"I'm doing all right, but there must be more to life than this, and I would like to explore more of what's available in the world." It involves a kind of . . . what I call . . . "inner-declaration," because it's getting in touch with yourself at a much richer level than you might have otherwise.

A. B. ✦ I like that line.

Dr. Stoller ✦ You're exposing yourself to a lot of people in a very intimate way. As it turns out very often, it does solve problems by helping people work through a lot of things, but it doesn't necessarily *go into them*. It's much more interested in the person and how people react, how he affects other people, what kind of intimate relationships he can develop, or might possibly be able to develop. The problems are sort of beside the point. A great many people come into the encounter group with problems. If we could eliminate all the people without problems. . . .

A. B. ✦ You wouldn't have anybody there.

Dr. Stoller ✦ And a lot of things that take place in the encounter group are therapeutic. That is, they do help people. But, the basic assumption is—*we can't dissolve your problem*.

A. B. ✦ You don't call an encounter group necessarily therapy.

Dr. Stoller ✦ It's an *experience*. I'm just as satisfied to kind of experience you, while you're in the group, and let you know how I feel about you, how I experience you. In fact, the assumption is that this is *much more* the *important material,* in the sense that we tell the person about himself as we experience him, rather than his coming in and telling us about himself. A lot of times people come into the group and say,

"Let me tell you about myself," and they start to tell about problems, and then they say, in a sense, "Now react to me," and they're really asking you to react to a version of themselves. The encounter group says, "No. We'll ignore that for the moment and concentrate on what we are experiencing with you." We're really saying, "Let *us* tell you about you."

A. B. ✦ You're trying to give someone a new dimension in self-awareness—not specific aid for specific problems.

Dr. Stoller ✦ Yes, yes. And I want people to be clear about these three different types of groups.

A. B. ✦ You're mostly involved with the encounter groups.

Dr. Stoller ✦ I originally started as a therapist, and then I became interested in group therapy, then in the encounter and sensitivity training, which is sort of another word for it. I began to become involved in these growth centers, like Esalen, and they started to spring up all around the country. These are centers that put on programs that reach people like myself to put on a marathon, to put on a workshop, to put on something which people then come to on their own because they are interested in experiencing this particular experience.

A. B. ✦ What made you progress from group therapy to encounter groups?

Dr. Stoller ✦ I was working in a mental hospital with very disturbed people and I saw people in terms of diagnosis of their particular illnesses. When I began to move out in the world in a different way, I gathered people together without any particular diagnosis at all. As people came together. . . .

A. B. ✦ Just normal neurotics . . . or more?

Dr. Stoller ✦ I found that the person whom I'd designated as schizophrenic in the hospital, for example, and treated in a very particular kind of way, I'd find coming into one of these groups with a quantity of undifferentiated people, where we didn't give him a *label* and he had a chance to interact with a full range of people. I found that these people were very different. . . .

A. B. ◆ But you might see the person in a mental hospital and the person walking around, with the *same* kind of symptoms.

Dr. Stoller ◆ Absolutely. It's amazing. To me the experience of what happens to these people when they are labeled with their illness and put into a setting which really focuses in on sick people, so that they become fixated ... some awful things happen to people when they get labeled that way.

I don't know anything about you, and I don't have any prejudgments about you, and I don't have a label for you, and I just allow myself to experience you. I begin to see a whole range of things inside of you that I wouldn't see if I had both my mind and your mind sort of locked in prejudgment.

A. B. ◆ What would be some of the things that you might see?

Dr. Stoller ◆ We began to see in the groups that people can open up to other people, they can allow themselves to be touched, they can reach over to other people; they really flowered in a way that I never saw—this with schizophrenics in hospitals. We never focused in on what's your problem, we just focused in on what you're like, what's your potential, and why do you hang back, and why don't you reach out to us, and sometimes we'd pick them up and rock them and hold them.

A. B. ◆ This was all spontaneous?

Dr. Stoller ◆ It was the merger of our feelings for the person. Maybe it wasn't spontaneous, but it was very applicable to the kinds of feelings we'd developed about the person. Maybe I would suggest it, but I'd only suggest it at a point where I felt very strongly that this was something I felt I would like to do. The person would be open to feelings in a way that I'd never seen before. I began to suspect that there was a beautiful way of helping people flower by focusing in on their *potential*— what is available to them that they're not using.

A. B. ◆ In other words, an ideal of what man might be.

Dr. Stoller ◆ A positive theme ... I think is a very relevant thing. We all have parts of ourselves that we haven't really made use of and these are things which I found much more

able to tune in with less defenses?

Dr. Stoller ◆ Some people think that the time wears away your defenses. However, I feel differently about the long period of time. My feeling is that we build up a momentum. It's almost like once you start to run, it takes a while to build up the speed, and it takes a while to build up an intensity of feeling about oneself, about the other people, and so that there is kind of a momentum that develops as we continue. Intense feelings get generated, people get involved . . . you know, as time goes on we become pretty important to one another. What happens then is that the world really recedes and the group becomes a world. Let's talk about the marathon. Literally you are in another world. The other world you came from disappears for the time being.

A. B. ◆ And you forget your relatives, friends, family?

Dr. Stoller ◆ The other recedes. Emotionally, this world becomes the world, and these things that are going on between you and the people become very important. This means that when you have a fight, some kind of a crisis, it really upsets you, really disturbs you, really gets under your skin. And this again is one of the very important things that happens in a marathon. People do get into crises with one another.

A. B. ◆ What's an example of a crisis?

Dr. Stoller ◆ A crisis is basically when you get back something from somebody that you don't want. In other words, if I get back negative feelings from you or I get back misunderstanding, that's not in line with what I intend to be getting from you. What we generally do is retreat; that is, I am hurt, and I go away, and the next time we get back together again, I'll be a little bit on my guard and won't allow myself to be hurt as readily as I had been in the past. This is how people in a sense handle their crises. In the marathon, they can't retreat. They have to stay with the person. They have to stay in the group. Instead of retreating, they find themselves involved with this person, they find themselves with their personal crisis.

A. B. ◆ Can you think of a crisis?

Dr. Stoller ◆ The most recent one was in a group that I just did, and it basically involved a girl who had been working with a physician in psychotherapy. She had become very, very trusting of him. She really didn't trust men at all, but she had become very trusting of him. Then she had to go to a hospital for a female operation, and found that she was really distrustful of the surgeon. She felt that he might do something to her, and she was very reluctant to go. It was really at her psychotherapist's urging and his saying that it would be all right that she finally went and had her operation. After the operation, she was having all kinds of pain which she had not anticipated. Someone said that she might not be able to have any children any more. This was one of the things that was running through her mind. All her trust was in the psychotherapist who had originally said to go ahead. It turned out in the marathon that this same man had withheld some information from *another* woman in the group. All this came out in the group.

A. B. ◆ So he showed some duplicity, humanness, too.

Dr. Stoller ◆ That's right, and for a valid reason, but this put the girl into utter panic. She felt that if her therapist was making a decision not to tell somebody else something, what cruelties could he be doing with her?

A. B. ◆ Did she cry? Did she scream? Did she sob?

Dr. Stoller ◆ This was a very hysterical scene in which she accused him of being untrusting, and it got into her feelings of not being a woman any more. It's all the feelings that almost anyone would feel in response to one of these female operations: "They've tampered with me and I don't know where I'm at."

A. B. ◆ How did this get resolved?

Dr. Stoller ◆ Nobody put her down or turned from her, and she had an opportunity to go through her feelings with the group.

When she came out on the other side—she had always reacted with a great deal of toughness—she came to the realization that she could reach out despite human imperfection and this was a beautiful emotional moment, this deep realization.

A. B. ✦ Does this feeling last? That kind of emotional catharsis?

Dr. Stoller ✦ The experience I've had is that they tend to. . . . In a sense it's not so much that they last. People have an experience. We were all dragged into this body and soul, so that she was with a group of people who were with her in a very profound way.

A. B. ✦ Maybe you're saying that if you experience that deeply, it *just is.*

Dr. Stoller ✦ That's right. It *just is,* and it's something that is in you. This doesn't mean that she's never going to be without doubts again. That's ludicrous. You can't live that way; nobody does. Everybody's full of doubts, and backsliding. But she's had *one* experience where people have stayed with her, which probably means a hell of a lot more than words, and which in the long run will sustain her. She may backslide.

A. B. ✦ But she'll remember. . . .

Dr. Stoller ✦ . . . more quickly, a little more trust in the future towards men.

A. B. ✦ Since this is so emotional, if people are near the edge of a psychotic break, could this be a dangerous experience?

Dr. Stoller ✦ I've had people who appear to be psychotic, or, I prefer to call it disorganized. It is possible. Now these are rare. There was a young chap who had to go to a hospital for a couple weeks and that upset the hell out of me. You know that's something I don't want to see happen. However, this is one person out of probably a few thousand, which is extraordinarily low. I've had a lot of training, I'm a clinical psychologist. I've had a lot of experience working with disturbed people and when somebody gets upset, I don't become frightened. I'm not afraid of people getting disturbed, upset, disorganized.

A. B. ◆ Just *anybody* should certainly not be running encounter groups.

Dr. Stoller ◆ I feel a lot of the bad reports come because leaders have become frightened. I think when I become frightened, I communicate that fear, and I think you and I are into some very bad vibrations.

A. B. ◆ I can understand that.

Dr. Stoller ◆ I'm scaring you by my fear, particularly if I'm a professional and a person who sets the tone. I've thought of some crazy things myself. There are times when I think I'm going crazy and I don't think it's so bad.

A. B. ◆ It all depends on how you look at it.

Dr. Stoller ◆ That's right. I think one of the devastating things that we do is get frightened of people who go crazy. When we get frightened we begin to do things to them instead of allowing them to go through it, *we* freeze them at *their* fear. I think people can go through it. Now if I'm able to stay with it, I'll be able to help them through that. Something very beautiful comes out of it, instead of something frightening. It's not the end of the world.

A. B. ◆ That's a very different look at going crazy!

I want to ask you about my fear of airplanes and, if I came to an encounter group, how you would help me. I have an awful fear of flying.

Dr. Stoller ◆ My initial reaction is that you just want to take care of your fear of airplanes per se; maybe you ought to go to behavior therapy. If you're interested in you as a person and how you affect the world and what you do to the world, I would say, "Come to the group." [One of my perceptions of where we are today doing a survey of a lot of different therapies is, that *there is no one single road.*] *That there are many roads and many ways to receive help for many different kinds of things.*

A. B. ◆ You sound like the introduction to my book.

Dr. Stoller ◆ I was at a point at which I thought I'd found a

truth. *This is it. The way to go.* Now it seems very ludicrous
to me. People are much more complicated, much richer than
that. And you know, if you have a fear of airplanes there are
ways to deal with that. That's not going to take care of all
aspects of your life, that's not going to give you the flavor of
your life. I think the group is much more apt to do that. There
are other situations where you might want to work, for
example, on something about your feelings, about your
mother. You may want to go into individual, long-term
therapy in which you become aware of that you have
unresolved feelings about your mother and these get in the
way. You might want to go into that kind of therapy.

A. B. ✦ Is there anything special or any special kind of problem
that encounter groups would be more right for than anything
else? Or would it just be this total awareness of a human
being in the world?

Dr. Stoller ✦ There is one particular kind of person for whom it
is very, very right. That is for the person who is isolated. Just
the person who would be afraid of that kind of approach. The
person who has trouble reaching out to people and allowing
himself to be touched by people.

A. B. ✦ Isn't it hard to get those people to go? I know right now
of someone who . . . it would be so right for her, but she
wouldn't go near one.

Dr. Stoller ✦ Some of them are, but a lot of them do reach out.
They come to the realization that, wow, this is what I need,
because a lot of it is really enjoyable. They begin to see this
and they begin to get hungry for it. There is no place to
experience people like the encounter group.

A. B. ✦ Is there any follow-up afterwards, or do I just sort of
disappear into the world again and never have any contact
with the group leader or with the group?

Dr. Stoller ✦ This depends entirely upon both the leader and the
person. The way I particularly run my groups—now various
people run them differently—I am available, but it depends on

you to come reach me rather than me to go reach you. A good 60 percent contact me one way or another. They phone me. They write me. We run into each other. They come back into my groups. What I have always found is that very often the particular kind of marathon groups that I run have set people off on a road of exploration where they are not interested in making contact with me necessarily . . . but one of the great benefits is that people are able to see their own strength without the necessity of finding one person to rely on. So what they often do is go off on a series of experiences—other kinds of groups, other kinds of workshops, other kinds of group leaders—and experience a whole set of things rather than trying to find a person or an approach of which they become enamored. I think that has a tendency to infantilize them in a way. You know, "I found this wonderful person who is going to do it for me." Then they have to unwork that in a way. They have to work themselves out of that kind of experience. I just ran into a girl who we had five years ago at Berkeley, a young student, and she was radiant, and I met her at a conference. She told me how much the experience meant to her and this had set her off in a whole course of other things, a whole series of things. She really looked delightful and full of a lot of life. I was terribly pleased that she had come to me, for me to be the one to lead her to all this.

A. B. • Quite different from traditional psychiatry.

Dr. Stoller • This really depends on the person much more. Traditional therapy says, "Come to me and I'll take you and I'll make you grow." This is a more adult kind of relationship.

A. B. • Where are encounter groups going?

Dr. Stoller • It's very obvious that encounter groups have hit a very important nerve in people's lives. It has to do with intimacy, it has to do with their ability to reach people. It's very clear that it's answering something very real in contemporary American life. In twenty years it may be not as relevant, and we may have to have some other form of treatment. I feel all these treatments, all these approaches are *very relevant to their time*. There's no such thing as an approach that is irrelevant to its time.

A. B.   •   The sense of alienation today is relevant to our time!

Dr. Stoller   •   The encounter group is extraordinarily relevant to contemporary America with its high degree of mobility, with its high degree of people who move at an extraordinary pace. I see American cities and American suburbs as places where people are isolated from one another. I think it's very important for us to realize why people reach out this way, and I think that this is the basic . . . I hate to call it a sickness, because this is not sickness, but this is the basic condition that man finds himself in today. The encounter group is one of the responses to it. It's really an experiment of people trying to find one another; it's not the total experiment, and there will be other ways in which people try to find one another, but this is a very important and very rich way in which they do it. And I've personally been very pleased to be part of this particular experiment. It's done a lot for me personally. I think I've seen a lot of people grow and become richer for the process, but that doesn't represent the total answer, either. I don't know what that is. I've been very struck by the fact that people look for *answers* . . . you know, they go into analysis for several years, and the theory is, "If I get this major engine overhauled, it will do the rest of my life." But it doesn't work that way.

9

Nude Marathon Therapy

Paul Bindrim

Paul Bindrim

is a licensed California psychologist, formerly on the faculty of El Camino College, and in private practice for some twenty years. He has long been an innovator in therapeutic methods, and has done research in ESP and the development of peak-oriented therapy procedures. Bindrim says, "In an age of alienation, nude marathons set the stage for a joyful human reunion."

Nude marathons are for any age; many men and women with physical handicaps—i.e., loss of arm or leg, or a mastectomy—have found that a nude marathon is helpful in the complete acceptance of a handicap.

Nude marathons provide a broad-spectrum learning-experience in an environment where it is safe to express the gamut of human emotion. Participants may arrange for private postsessions, and a group postsession is included as part of the marathon experience. These are designed to help participants trust their new awareness.

Paul Bindrim, who developed this technique, travels throughout the United States to major growth centers, where he conducts these marathons. He publishes a newsletter, and has done a film and written several articles on the nude marathon.

Adelaide Bry ◆ Paul Bindrim, you are the originator of the nude marathon as a form of therapy. How did you start?

Mr. Bindrim ◆ In some encounter groups, emotional intimacy developed to a point that the members spontaneously disrobed. Naturally, we began to wonder what would happen if members disrobed *first*, and then interacted.

A. B. ◆ What did you find?

Mr. Bindrim ◆ The whole process of becoming emotionally open and intimate is hastened and intensified by nudity.

A. B. ◆ What is the basic idea of the nude marathon?

Mr. Bindrim ◆ The major idea is to combine the warm water of the pool with nudity and massage to enable the person to reexperience the very early periods of his life.

A. B. ◆ *Who* is doing all this massaging?

Mr. Bindrim ◆ The whole group concentrates on one person, and we also give him a bottle and rock him.

A. B. ◆ A baby bottle?

Mr. Bindrim ◆ Yes. A lactating cotherapist would be better, but since we don't have one we simply use a bottle. We recreate the environment of infancy by rocking the person in warm water where he is weightless and can regress to this prelanguage time of life.

A. B. ◆ Grownups behave *just like babies again.* Sounds frightening.

Mr. Bindrim ◆ It's wonderful. The massage results in the regression, and this result I consider more important than the other effects of nudity, such as improving an individual's body-image or self-image, or enabling one to talk out sexual blocks.

A. B. ◆ Just all those nude bodies must produce something in itself.

Mr. Bindrim ◆ The merging of people into a kind of total humanness is an answer to alienation.

A. B. ◆ Can just *one* twenty-hour experience change someone's basic feelings and outlook on life?

Mr. Bindrim ◆ Absolutely. But you spend a considerable amount of the time enabling a person to reach that kind of openness and trust that he knew as a baby. So much trauma has its origin in that prelanguage era of life. Once this new attitude of trust is established, the work has just begun. It may also take the person some time to reshape his lifestyle to fit his new values.

A. B. ◆ Are you saying this is right for everyone?

Mr. Bindrim ◆ No, I'm not saying it is a cure-all. But I have a hunch this is a more potent way of getting people into this early state than we have had before, and thus releasing them from the past and freeing them to express more fully in the present.

A. B. ◆ Let's start at the beginning of a nude marathon. What happens?

Mr. Bindrim ◆ Between fourteen and eighteen people attend a session. They arrive about seven in the evening; they introduce themselves and then we have eyeball contact followed by physical interaction. That is, we look directly into each other's eyes at close range. Then we permit ourselves to respond physically. This could mean hugging, wrestling, or any kind of interaction that occurs spontaneously. All of this happens without any talking and leads to a feeling of closeness. We then talk for a little while about our anxieties about nudity. Then everyone disrobes.

A. B. ◆ Is it light or dark?

Mr. Bindrim ◆ It is dark, we are playing music, and everyone is asked to keep their eyes closed while walking in a small circle. We permit skin contact to happen, neither avoiding nor encouraging it. So we get everyone used to skin contact and nudity, without making an issue out of looking or exposing.

A. B. ◆ What about talking at this point?

Mr. Bindrim ◆ We don't, but we do ask them to hum a note, and this results in a meditationlike turn-on. Everyone quickly has the feeling of being all part of one human mass.

A. B. ◆ How early in the marathon does this happen?

Mr. Bindrim ◆ Within the first four hours. Basically, I conceive of the first half of the marathon as a means of producing a good functioning group in the nude. This phase is like any group encounter with the addition of nudity.

A. B. ◆ When do the people become unconscious of being nude?

Mr. Bindrim ◆ Almost as soon as they *are* nude, if these procedures are followed. If a group were not properly prepared in dead silence. We want to improve communication through for nudity, they might well wind up just looking at each other increased intimacy, not kill it. Ideational communication usually isn't very intimate; audiovisual is more intimate (i.e., seeing and hearing), skin contact is even more intimate, and emotional relatedness is more intimate than that.

A. B. ◆ Anything beyond that as a goal?

Mr. Bindrim ◆ Yes, the final dimension is a peak experience as defined by Maslow (former President of the American Psychological Association). This is a spiritual experience of total union. It goes beyond sexual union which is genitally focused, and carries with it a sense of joy and aliveness.

A. B. ◆ What else do you do to help them accept their nudity?

Mr. Bindrim ◆ We have many procedures. In one, everyone is in a circle, legs in the air, looking through their legs at each other. While in this exposed posture, they relate anything that they have done sexually that has left them with a feeling of guilt.

A. B. ◆ That sounds *both weird* and *funny!*

Mr. Bindrim ◆ You soon realize that the head end and the tail end are indispensable parts of the same person, and that one end is about as good as the other. This phase is quite humorous, not only because of the unusual posture, but also because of the exaggerated sense of guilt and the relief that comes when the group still accepts the participant despite his terrible secrets. It is important for us to accept our entire body. For example, one young overweight woman who would never appear in public in a bathing suit learned to accept her body at a nude marathon. Her improved self-concept changed her entire life style. She stopped using narcotics, gave up her promiscuous sex life with its attendant unwanted pregnancies, returned to college and discovered her talent in art, dated professional men, and is now engaged.

A. B. ◆ Have you pretty much described the first part of the marathon?

Mr. Bindrim ◆ Yes, and it should be understood that this first part is varied to suit the needs of the group, while the second half in the water is not variable. By now it is four in the morning and I hope that the nude group is functioning as well as might be expected of a clothed group: in other words, that they are no longer a crowd, but a group of people relating to one another in a relatively honset fashion.

A. B. ◆ Of course, there's always a lot of giggling by nonserious people about a nude marathon. But you did say in an article in *Psychology Today* that society was not ready for sex in the nude marathon. What did you mean by that?

Mr. Bindrim ◆ Professional organizations, like the American Psychological Association, are quite conservative and are concerned about their image. If I permitted sexual expression in my sessions, it would probably cost me my membership regardless of the scientific value of the experiment, or the possible benefit to the public. Without the backing of Abraham Maslow, the President of the Association, (now deceased) it is doubtful that I could have run nude marathons and now be a member in good standing. Loss of membership would seriously hamper the communication of these ideas at conventions and in journals, and their acceptance and exploration by other professionals.

A. B. ✦ How would you use sex, if you could?

Mr. Bindrim ✦ If I were free to experiment with overt sexuality, I could only tell you how I would use it after I had experimented. In this area most a priori conclusions are questionable. Our society has restricted and overemphasized sex so thoroughly that this preconditioning would have to be overcome before one could expect to relinquish all controls and trust to open communication and the natural dynamic of the group. Two psychologists in Los Angeles ran a sexually unrestricted group for swingers, with disappointing results. According to one of them, the people who attended came primarily to get plugged into each other, and this attitude resulted in little else of significance occurring. Just sex, no feelings!

A. B. ✦ Your marathon has a format—after everyone takes their clothes off, what happens next?

Mr. Bindrim ✦ We form a circle around one lit candle and meditate, with the help of a recording by Alan Watts. We each have a glass which we fill from one bottle of wine. During these next four hours we meditate or sleep. (Everyone is asked to bring a sleeping bag to the marathon.) Our silent period has begun.

A. B. ✦ How long does the silence last?

Br. Bindrim ✦ Until 2:00 P.M. the next afternoon. Four hours after the silence begins we wake everyone with a Brandenburg concerto . . . and have a very light breakfast. We then go down to the pool, which is heated to body temperature (98.6) so that it resembles the womb.

A. B. ✦ What is the therapeutic reason for silence?

Mr. Bindrim ✦ By eliminating language we encourage regression to infancy. A baby doesn't understand language, but he does understand sighs and tears and emotional expressions.

If you're raging and someone else rages, this is emotionally reassuring and lets you rage even more. A person saying, "Feel free to get angry," would not have the same effect. We find that empathy is so much better expressed without words that by the time the group returns to the use of language they wish they could be silent again.

A. B. ✦ How does the nonverbal communication in the pool work?

Mr. Bindrim ✦ Everyone forms two parallel rows in the pool, just like a conveyor belt, and each participant is rocked gently and passed right on down the row. It's a fantastic experience to see humanity passing right under your nose that way. And when you're being passed there's so much tenderness and love in that touch that all the hurts that are inside you just well up and you break down and cry. All hell breaks loose, and it all happens without words.

A. B. ✦ But is it always *tears*, never *laughter?*

Mr. Bindrim ✦ Yes, usually it's tears. It's the feeling of needing to love and to be loved that finds expression. But, of course, not everyone breaks down. Those that do experience this closeness which they lack. There it is, it's possible, it's the potential of a greater life, yet they are living lives of isolated aloneness, of quiet desperation. It's so releasing to feel this, it feels so great, that by contrast, the lack of it hurts so much. It's like seeing pictures of home when you're potentially homesick and trying to cover it up.

A. B. ✦ It sounds tremendous for one experience, but you . . . you do this so often. Does it lose its impact for you?

Mr. Bindrim ✦ Oh, no. I live out there in an alienated world, too. It's good to see and feel this warmth, and to help others rediscover it in their relationships.

A. B. ✦ What happens after the conveyor belt?

Mr. Bindrim ✦ We ask each person to create dynamic tension in his body and hyperventilate.

A. B. ✦ Is this still in the pool?

Mr. Bindrim ✦ Yes, standing in very shallow water. When you have done this for a while, you lie down on your back in the water, and maybe eight or nine people will cluster around holding and rocking you. At this point most participants begin to cry. We then massage the tight muscles in the stomach, particularly the ones that hurt because they are being held tense. We also massage the muscles in the neck, jaw, and face.

A. B. ✦ You mean one person massages another?

Mr. Bindrim ✦ No, not just one. *Everyone* works on one person at the same time; one person will be working on his stomach, another on the head, four more will be holding his arms and legs so he can rage, scream, and strike out like a baby without doing any damage. We may have eight people working on one person at one time.

A. B. ✦ Sounds great for the ego as well as the body.

Mr. Bindrim ✦ We alternate massaging and rocking the participant. During the rocking everyone puts his head against the person so that his entire skin is covered with loving touch. His favorite music is played, his favorite smells are present, and he is given a bottle.

A. B. ✦ Beautiful . . . like babyhood at its best.

Mr. Bindrim ✦ It really is. Remember that expression about keeping a stiff upper lip, which really means don't break down and cry? Upper lips are, at times, kept stiff to prevent crying, but there are many muscles as well which we keep stiff in order to hold back various kinds of emotion. By massaging these muscles vigorously in the warmth of the pool, they can be helped to relax, and the repressed emotions released.

A. B. ✦ It's as easy as that?

Mr. Bindrim ✦ The initial effect when you massage a stiff muscle is a certain amount of physical pain. As the emotion that is being held back by the muscle tension comes into expression, the muscle relaxes and the physical pain lessens as the emotional pain is experienced. The person may have fantasies of painful events that occurred very early in life corresponding to these emotional traumas.

A. B. ✦ Do you mean that people have actually told you of memory recall at a preverbal age, based upon their experience at the nude marathon?

Mr. Bindrim ✦ Yes, they have. They've told me of experiences as babies, and even birth experiences.

A. B. ✦ Your enthusiasm, the feeling in your voice, that alone is so wonderful when you talk about it.

Mr. Bindrim ✦ It is a wonderful experience to take human beings, all strangers to one another, and develop this feeling of closeness by bringing them back to a greater awareness of their origins, to what some have even called a Garden of Eden experience, a feeling of closeness with all mankind.

A. B. ✦ This sounds like experiences that people have with LSD. Is there any similarity?

Mr. Bindrim ✦ Yes, it resembles the LSD experience in many respects, but has the advantage of being free of the dangers inherent in the drug. It results from human warmth and closeness and is somewhat transferable to the daily life of the participant. One psychiatrist, who is on the staff of an organization doing LSD research in the United States, and who has supervised over 1,600 sessions, on attending a nude marathon said that the effect resembled at least 125 to 150 grams of LSD.

A. B. ✦ How does it affect people who have been on drugs?

Mr. Bindrim ✦ Some discover that they can have the same trip without drugs and that it is natural. They no longer feel that drugs are the only route to this kind of experience. They are then able to control their use of drugs and many give them up entirely.

A. B. ✦ Does this turn-on, with its joy and aliveness, carry over into life when the participant leaves the group?

Mr. Bindrim ✦ To some degree it does and to some degree it is lost. When the participant learns to be emotionally open in the group this is a new experience. It also gives him the capacity to discriminate between emotionally open and more tightly closed individuals in life. However, his life circumstances will still be the same as when he entered the group. This will tend to turn him off unless he reorganizes his lifestyle to fit his new value-system.

A. B.   ✦   Aside from a normal turn-on, how does this affect the sex lives of average persons?

Mr. Bindrim   ✦   A high percentage of them say that their sexual enjoyment and the frequency of contact has increased since the session, that it has been liberating.

A. B.   ✦   How do you explain this in view of the fact that you don't permit sexual expression in the session? I would imagine that it could have an inhibiting effect.

Mr. Bindrim   ✦   Although it may seem strange that participants who are not permitted to have sexual relationships during the session should report increased sexual enjoyment following the session, this can be understood when we realize that many Americans are not only inhibited sexually but inhibited sensually as well.

A. B.   ✦   What is the difference?

Mr. Bindrim   ✦   The pleasure of physical contact is sensuality. When it is focused in the genital area I define it as sexuality. The two are often associated with each other and confused. For example, when a dance therapist asked girls to walk across the room sensuously they were unable to do it. However, when she suggested that they walk across the room acting like prostitutes they could do it with ease. They could not conceive of themselves as being sensual without this meaning sexual and immoral as well. When women learn that they can be sensual without necessarily winding up in bed, they become more attractive. Sensuality adds to the beauty of a woman and in no way stops her from saying, "no." In the nude marathon where sensuality is encouraged and sexuality is inhibited, the two become clearly separated and the participant learns that he can be sensual without necessarily involving himself sexually.

A. B. ✦ Does this also apply to men?

Mr. Bindrim ✦ Sensuality between men is even more strongly inhibited than between men and women, and yet it is the main medium through which love is expressed. As a result our male population is trained to be aggressive, competitive, and hostile, and is inhibited in terms of expressing love. Sensuality is associated with sexuality, and males who hug or touch are considered to be homosexual. The nude marathon has a freeing effect, and some men on returning home and carrying this newfound freedom into their relationships with their sons have had their boys look at them and say, "Daddy, are you ill?" A judge in the Juvenile Court once remarked that in all of his time on the bench, he has never seen a father put his arm around a boy who was in trouble.

A. B. ✦ How about people who are inhibited sexually and have little contact with the opposite sex?

Mr. Bindrim ✦ It is hard to remain fearful of the opposite sex when you have continuous nude contact with them for almost twenty hours. This has resulted in impotent males becoming potent, and repressed and withdrawn individuals beginning to associate with the opposite sex in a normal manner. Even sexual exhibitionists of long standing have been cured of their symptoms.

A. B. ✦ Wouldn't these sessions tend to make people more promiscuous sexually?

Mr. Bindrim ✦ No. In general, they have the reverse effect. For example, eleven members of the Sexual Freedom League attended one session. In the course of the session they discovered the pleasures of emotional intimacy, which are deeper and more meaningful than impersonal sexual expression. At the follow-up session a month later, all but one said that he preferred sex with *emotion* to the *impersonal* kind experienced at an orgy. They had given up much of their promiscuity, and had paired up in couples and small groups. Impersonality had given way to ongoing relationships.

A. B. ✦ Have married couples ever attended your sessions? I would imagine that they would be quite jealous of each other under the permissive circumstances that apparently prevail.

Mr. Bindrim ✦ Yes, they do attend, and they are jealous. Perhaps one of the most common conflicts in marriage is the desire to be close and the desire to be free. However, the circumstances that threaten closeness are far fewer than most couples imagine. For example, few couples realize that sensual attraction to others is quite transient and does not threaten a close emotional relationship. When these conflicts are faced openly as they are in the nude marathon, they are resolved to a far greater degree than in normal life-circumstances, where they are frequently hidden. The end result is often a greater latitude of freedom and a greater sense of security in the relationship.

A. B. ✦ Have you actually had persons attend your sessions who have been physically deformed? For example, women with mastectomies?

Mr. Bindrim ✦ Yes, indeed I have. These are some of the simplest conditions to help. Generally, the psychological handicap is greater than the physical, but the person who has undergone the injury or operation seldom realizes it. For instance, many women, after having a breast amputated, wear falsies. They withdraw from close relationships with men, making the assumption that if a man ever found out that instead of a breast, they had a scar, they would be rejected on the spot. Only when they have participated in the group and have discovered that while the first reaction is surprise, this soon gives way to about the same kind of acceptance they have always known.

A. B. ✦ But all of our defects aren't real. Some are imagined. How about people who think that their genitals are too small or that their breasts are misshaped, or the many other things people can feel are wrong with their bodies?

Mr. Bindrim ✦ These conditions are fairly easy to treat in a nude session. Once the part is exposed and the group gives their honest reaction, the participant's opinion is frequently changed.

A. B. ✦ But aren't most people rather ugly with their clothing off? Particularly older people?

Mr. Bindrim ✦ No, on the contrary. Our face ages more than our body because it reflects the strain of our long continued emotional stress. As a result, when people become undressed, even the aged, in general, look younger and better than they did with clothing on.

A. B. ✦ How do you know what happens to these people after they leave your sessions? For instance, how do you know that they don't commit suicide or have other drastic side-effects?

Mr. Bindrim ✦ I hold a follow-up session one month after the marathon to evaluate the changes that have taken place. In the course of conducting over fifty marathons, I know of no instance in which there has been a serious deleterious result. No one has become psychotic and had to be hospitalized, or committed suicide, or murder, or any similar kind of drastic behavior.

A. B. ✦ What kind of people come to your sessions?

Mr. Bindrim ✦ These sessions draw a large spectrum of people from every walk of life. In general, they come from the higher financial and educational brackets than would be expected at clothed marathons. For instance, at one session we had a schoolteacher, an artist, a college professor, an editor of a magazine, a celibate Catholic priest, two housewives, two students, a physician, a mail carrier, and a person who was unemployed. Almost all of these individuals come as a result of personal referral, and about 50 per cent are sent by psychiatrists and clinical psychologists.

A. B. ✦ I have a fear of airplanes so strong that I have

physiological symptoms whenever I fly. How can you help me?

Mr. Bindrim ✦ I understand that many airplane pilots, when attempting to go from propeller-driven planes to jet planes, have experienced similar problems. Many of them have washed out and have had to find new careers. If I viewed your condition as an airline might that of one of its valued pilots, the goal of our interaction would be the elimination of the fear and the physiological symptoms so that you would be able to function effectively when flying in airplanes. In this respect, I am informed that the airlines have used behavioral therapists to treat their pilots and have had good results. If symptom-control were our sole objective, I would refer you to a behavioral therapist.

On the other hand, since most individuals who have had a successful growth experience report that their presenting symptom was only a small part of the real problem (like the part of an iceberg that is visible above water), I would discuss this matter with you and suggest that you attend a nude marathon. I would suggest that you be open-minded and accept growth in any area rather than specifically focusing on the presenting symptom. I would also suggest that your fear of airplanes might well disappear as a result of a broader area of growth that might occur during these sessions. While I would be interested in knowing some of your past history, if it were available in an easily readable form, I would not bother running tests or require preliminary individual screening sessions.

A. B. ✦ I would just come to the marathon and see for myself?

Mr. Bindrim ✦ In the marathon you would be surrounded by a thoroughly supporting group of warm and loving individuals. While this would not be the case when we first met and were all strangers, by the next morning you could count on this kind of atmosphere. Like a child who falls down and is hurt but holds back his crying until he reaches the security of his mother's arms, you would probably begin to feel your own hurt most keenly when the group began to provide this kind of loving atmosphere. At this point I would expect your emotional traumas to spontaneously surface so that there would be no need to search for them and pry them loose.

A. B. ◆ By morning I'm emotionally nude, too!

Mr. Bindrim ◆ Let's assume your fear is really giving up control and trusting that others will take care of your welfare. After all, in a plane your life depends upon everyone from the pilots to the mechanics that have serviced the craft, to the persons in the control tower, to the men who have forecast the weather, to personnel operating guidance systems, none of whom you either know or have much opportunity to persuade to take good care of you. Enclosed in the cabin and strapped in your seat, you are indeed helpless and dependent, even though you may be sipping your martini and assuring yourself that you are a fortunate and important member of society. If you cannot trust others and are a controlling kind of individual, these circumstances might indeed cause physiological symptoms.

A. B. ◆ How would I show this in the nude marathon?

Mr. Bindrim ◆ At the beginning this lack of trust might very well result in social game-playing, the cocktail-hour type thing; or, since your field is writing, perhaps a feigned interest in other people's problems designed primarily to keep the group from knowing anything about you. If they did by chance discover one of your secrets or inner feelings, you might react defensively, and in one way or another try to extricate yourself from a circumstance in which others might get to know you well enough so that your method of control would no longer work.

A. B. ◆ What might I feel then?

Mr. Bindrim ◆ You might feel the same physiological symptoms that happen when you fly. A sense of no longer having your feet on the ground, of no longer being able to take care of your own welfare. Instead of comforting you with a martini and a reassuring smile as a stewardess might do, I would suggest that you take the *risk* of feeling the symptom more intensely. I would assure you that you cannot understand it intellectually but can only go into it deeper by feeling it more intensely.

A. B. ◆ I can almost feel what you're asking me to feel.

Mr. Bindrim ◆ I would ask you to see that you were experiencing the same reaction on land that you normally experienced in the air, and that this was not merely a fear of airplanes but had wider significance. I would try to help you to see how you're limiting your life at this very moment by withdrawing rather than trusting the group and letting the symptoms happen. However, the choice to carry this further or not, would at all times be left up to you.

A. B. ◆ You mean if an anxiety is too intense, the person can stop.

Mr. Bindrim ◆ Absolutely. But your fear of trusting might become apparent the moment we became nude. You might be the only person crouched in the corner with a towel covering you. Symbolically exposing your body might mean exposing yourself emotionally and no longer being able to avoid or control human contact. Whatever the circumstances under which these symptoms occurred, I would ask you to *intensify* them and I would help you to intensify them by doing whatever proved helpful. For example, I might see that you were rocking back and forth gently as you spoke. In this case we would pick you up, hold you in our arms, and rock you. This experience might prove very threatening. If you're a person exercising rigid control, you might be afraid that we would drop you. You would be unable to relax. You would be holding on. Your airplane symptoms would become ever more intense. As we rocked you, we would give you full skin contact all over your body so that you would feel close to us. As we increased the warm, receptive, and inviting circumstances that encourage you to let go, you would become increasingly aware of your tendency to hang on and control.

A. B. ◆ Sounds beautiful and unreal, both.

Mr. Bindrim ◆ Strangely enough, the greater the security, the more your symptoms might intensify, since the security itself would be challenging you to take the very risk of letting go which you are afraid of. To further heighten the effect, we might play your favorite music, and if you like incense or perfume, someone would hold a burning piece of it where you could smell the aroma.

A. B. ◆ There must be some physical signs of my anxiety by now.

Mr. Bindrim ◆ As your symptoms became more intense, I might see that your fists were clenching. I would ask you to become aware of them and to feel what they want to do. If your fists began to thrash and punch, I would hold cushions where you could hit them and encourage you to let go *even more*. If your eyes were open, I would ask you to close them and tell me if you saw anything as you went deeper into the experience. At this point you might suddenly see the face of your mother who died when you were four years of age and quickly hold back the fists that were wildly punching a moment before. You might express an ambivalent need to be loved by her and to strike out at her.

A. B. ◆ There seems a prescribed pattern as the marathon progresses.

Mr. Bindrim ◆ A general direction—as we ask you to express your feelings. First loving and caressing and then hitting. When you were expressing love, a woman in the group would allow you to caress her nude body and when you struck out there would be a cushion to absorb your blows. You would probably find that it was difficult to hit and when you finally accomplished this, you might discover that deep in your heart you resented her for leaving you by dying. As you realized that this was childish, your fury and rage might well be replaced by forgiveness. You might cry and again feel the kind of love and trust that you felt for her before she passed on. The physiological symptoms would now leave you and in all probability not return.

A. B. ◆ You have to face a lot of violent emotion all at once in a nude marathon.

Mr. Bindrim ◆ If in the early stage of the marathon you did not, we might hope that when the silence began and you could no longer distract yourself, you would then experience these feelings. By morning when I asked you to lie down in the warm water of the swimming pool and be rocked, this would be an even more potent invitation to let go and trust than you experienced the previous evening when you were held and rocked. Perhaps you would still lie in our arms like a stiff board, well protected within your defensive muscle-armor despite the body temperature water of the pool, the silence, the nonverbal expression of sighs and human emotion, the weightlessness, the skin contact, the helplessness as you were held by other persons, the freedom to scream without inhibition and to kick and to thrash without responsibility, the bottle of milk, and your favorite music and smells. At first you might even struggle with the people who were rocking you. Perhaps you would try to sit up instead of lying down. The fear that you knew in the airplane might well return and now be associated with drowning. It might be hard for you to trust them to keep your head above water. Your need to control might well block your capacity to receive and respond to the love of the group. And yet you are still being challenged to *take that risk and let go.*

A. B. ◆ Suppose I still can't?

Mr. Bindrim ◆ In order to keep holding back and maintaining control, muscles throughout your body would be in tension. Your arms might ache since your fists both wanted to strike at your mother and hold back from striking at her, thus producing a cramp. Muscle tension would be apparent in your stomach. While you were being held by the group, I would be massaging these areas. You would feel pain and perhaps painful emotion. This massaging would be alternated with warmth, rocking, love, and closeness. Finally, these feelings would become overwhelming. You would no longer be able to hold back and stay in control. As you began to let go, to thrash and to scream, the images of your mother might well recur and a sequence similar to one that might have happened on the previous evening would happen now. You would probably experience the fear you might experience if your plane began suddenly to fall. But now you would be free to express it. If you were still not able to scream and were still holding back by clenching your jaws, someone at your head would begin massaging your jaw muscles so that they would relax and no longer hold back. Since other persons before you would have screamed freely, you would know that it was perfectly acceptable to let your emotions out in their fullest form.

A. B. ◆ I begin to feel the permission in your description.

Mr. Bindrim ◆ Between the outer permissiveness and the inner need your fear would finally be expressed with full intensity, using your entire body. Early scenes of childhood might recur. You might go back to times before your mother died, when you also felt the loss of support and security—perhaps when you rolled out of a crib, or perhaps even earlier than that, during your birth. Conceivably you might even experience your own birth with a sense of being trapped in the vaginal canal. Suddenly you would understand the origin of the fear you felt in the long vagina-like cabin of the plane where you were so helpless. Repeatedly, we would massage and comfort you and then do whatever was necessary to bring you into contact with these fears again. Since in the present situation there would be no actual physical danger, these fears would gradually diminish. *You would learn that while at times it is desirable to control, at others it is desirable to be trusting and receptive.*

A. B. ◆ The drama is intense now! What next?

Mr. Bindrim ◆ At this point, you might be given a bottle of milk and discover that it was the sweetest milk that you had ever tasted. And as you sucked it in you would begin to feel the nourishment that comes to you from human love. You would feel in an overwhelming way your need to love and be loved. You would learn that the group loved you in your helpless, exposed, raw, and vulnerable state, and that this had *nothing* to do with your persuading or controlling them.

A. B. ◆ I have to be reduced so—in order to understand?

Mr. Bindrim ◆ If you want to reestablish the trust and the confidence that you need to function effectively. Later in the session I would discuss all of this with you and ask you to relate it to your lifestyle. As you look back on your fear of flying, you may now realize that your inability to trust was cheating you out of some of the deepest joys of living, of which flying was the *least* important.

Your new capacity to trust might express itself in greater emotional warmth. The group might tell you that you looked ten years younger. If you were married but living in a rather guarded kind of relationship, when you returned home your husband might tell you how open and warm you were. This might well induce him to open up in the same way, and perhaps you would talk all night long as you have never talked before. Or perhaps the trust would show itself in your work relationships.

A month later you would come to a postsession. Perhaps in the meantime the new perspective on your way of life would make many decisions and changes necessary. You might want to have a few private sessions with me in order to discuss these.

A. B. ◆ If, as you say, this is the real meaning of my fear of flying, would just one nude marathon change me?

Mr. Bindrim ◆ Possibly the first two or three nude marathons that you attended would only increase your capacity to trust to a minor degree until the fourth or fifth one resulted in a major breakthrough. Or perhaps you would be less fortunate and unresponsive.

At the worst, you would probably be as well off as when you began except for the loss of time and money. In both instances, these losses would be far less than what you might have risked losing in another form of psychotherapy.